CHOICES

CHOICES

A POST-ROE ABORTION RIGHTS MANIFESTO

MERLE HOFFMAN

Skyhorse Publishing

Skyhorse Publishing books may be purchased in bulk at special discounts for sales promotion, corporate gifts, fund-raising, or educational purposes. Special editions can also be created to specifications. For details, contact the Special Sales Department, Skyhorse Publishing, 307 West 36th Street, 11th Floor, New York, NY 10018 or info@skyhorsepublishing.com.

Skyhorse® and Skyhorse Publishing® are registered trademarks of Skyhorse Publishing, Inc.®, a Delaware corporation.

Visit our website at www.skyhorsepublishing.com.

Please follow our publisher Tony Lyons on Instagram @tonylyonsisuncertain

10 9 8 7 6 5 4 3 2 1

Library of Congress Control Number: 2023915524

Cover design by Brian Peterson

ISBN: 978-1-5107-7679-1
Ebook ISBN: 978-1-5107-7695-1

Printed in the United States of America

Portions of this book have appeared in slightly different form in print in *On The Issues Magazine: The Progressive Women's Quarterly* and online at https://ontheissuesmagazine.com/.

For Helen,
My first patient and catalyst of my calling.

"The best protection any woman can have is courage."
—Elizabeth Cady Stanton

CONTENTS

A Note about Language   ix

Introduction   xi

Chapter 1: The Roads Taken   1

Chapter 2: *Roe v. Wade* and Choices   13

Chapter 3: A Women's Rights State of Emergency   25

Chapter 4: The Rise of the Antis   53

Chapter 5: *Roe* Overturned   75

Chapter 6: Rising Up   95

Chapter 7: Resistance and Revolution   129

Chapter 8: Leadership and Power   157

Chapter 9: Passing the Torch   181

Chapter 10: Love   203

Epilogue: The Abyss Gazes Back   207

Acknowledgments   211

A NOTE ABOUT LANGUAGE

I understand and respect that not every person with the capacity for pregnancy identifies as a woman. I respect each individual's gender identity, expression, and experience, and desire to be helpful and compassionate to all who need information about abortion or support. As an expression of this concern, Choices Women's Medical Center initiated the first Trans Health Care Program in New York State in 2016.

While I do make an effort to use gender-inclusive language (person/people/they/them/patient) throughout this book, I do of course use woman/women/girls. I do so in order to acknowledge the long history of gender discrimination targeting women, the specialized health care that we provide, our experience with hundreds of thousands of women using our services, and the biological reality that only people with uteruses are biologically capable of become pregnant and carrying a fetus.

INTRODUCTION

A Candle Burning at Both Ends

The police officer held me back as I desperately tried to get inside. But even as I strained against him, I realized it was futile. I knew they were gone. Images of my cats—Sappho, Nietzsche, and Piaf—terrified, racing to find the closest corner, the safest spot, the spot that would become their little graves, crowded my mind. A local newspaper would later report that it took "over one hundred fire-fighters from seven departments"[1] some six hours to put the fire out. By the end of the night, my house—and everything that was inside—had been reduced to ashes.

As the flames surrounded my home and the explosions ripped into the air, I wasn't thinking about my other things—the paintings, the letters, all the detritus of years of travel writing and collecting. I succumbed to the inevitability of the whole terrible scene and watched in horrified silence. It occurred to me that it was January 1. A new year. A fresh start. Almost intuitively, I started doing the familiar work of loss.

This was a practice that I was skilled at, one I had started honing when I was three or four years old. As a child, when I would lose one of a pair of something I would consciously tell myself that I never had it in the first place. It was only many decades later that I learned that this was one of the first important lessons of the lived practice of Stoicism, the understanding that everything—all material reality—is fleeting, and that one must "practice" dying. Even

---

1 Taylor K. Vecsey, "FBI Interested in East Hampton Fire," *East Hampton Star*, January 8, 2015, https://www.easthamptonstar.com/archive/fbi-interested-east -hampton-fire.

with all the animals I have lost and put down over the years, the material loss of these three little creatures was searing.

But I wasn't thinking of my childhood in that moment, or the Stoics, or even—consciously—of loss. I was thinking of rebuilding. That home was, in many ways, the physical representation of my consciousness. I worked closely with the architects, designed almost everything inside and out. I made thousands of little decisions. It was so much *me*. And now it was incinerated before my eyes. It was a moment of absolute presence.

I have found myself thinking of that New Year's Day eight years ago more frequently since June 14, 2022, when the Supreme Court issued the decision that stripped women of the right to legal, safe abortion nationwide. Unlike so many others, I expected it, but I was not prepared for the reality of the loss, nor for the death of my life's work. A half century, gone.

I am now looking at those fifty years—my life, my vision and work, all the women whose hands I held during their abortions, all the challenges, battles, creative growth, political actions, women coming and rising together, the birth of the women's health movement—as a burning moment in time.

As if Edna St. Vincent Millay's candle burning at both ends— "it will not last the night/but ah, my foes, and oh, my friends/it gives a lovely light"—was encompassing all of us. And I am asking myself: How will we view those years? Will we appreciate them the way someone does when they only realize what they had once it's gone? Will we look back and ask, "Did you know there was a time when women in this country had fundamental civil human and constitutional rights?" Are we already normalizing our loss? Will we use *Roe* as a *standard* for what we are fighting for now? Will it be the floor of our future expectations? Will we demand even more—move up the ceiling of our vision? Or will we compromise and capitulate, already so comfortable in that position?

Two days after the fire, I was deep in the process of meeting with representatives of the FBI, which was investigating whether or not it was caused by arson. I was talking to insurance companies. And I was working with architects to redesign and rebuild.

It took me two years to do it. Now, after *Dobbs*, we must all ask ourselves: Will we normalize this second-class citizenship? Or will we rise up from the ashes and rubble stronger than before?

The Leak

I predicted the outcome of *Dobbs v. Jackson Women's Health Organization* the moment I read that the Supreme Court agreed to hear the case. Before the leak, before the media suddenly focused its attention on the issue, before anyone was even talking about it, I knew it was coming and I knew what it meant—the end of *Roe*. A catastrophe. As soon as I knew, I began making calls to people I had known for years, many of whom I had worked with. I called the leader of one of the major pro-choice groups in New York City and I asked, "What are we going to do about this? It's an emergency." The response was, "What emergency?" Obviously, the decision was going to come down, I said. And it would be devastating.

"Well, there are various issues we're working on," I was told. "We're working on this." "We're working on that." I couldn't believe what I was hearing.

The impending Supreme Court decision—which would decimate *Roe v. Wade* and strip away the constitutionally protected right to an abortion—was clearly not being taken seriously enough. People were not seeing how dangerous it was going to be, never mind the fact that we were looking at a theocratic, fascist takeover of the Supreme Court. The decision, to my mind, would be illegitimate.

As far as I could see, no one was out there saying, "This is coming. We have to get ready." Instead, a kind of preemptive post-*Roe* strategic thinking was bubbling up. *If they ban abortion in certain states*, the thinking went, *how do we raise money to pay for women to travel?* Or, *we have to get the pills to everyone.* To me, this was nothing short of a surrender. People were lying down before the battle had even begun. At the time, the public silence on this looming disaster was absolute and horrifying.

I did not sit long with this knowledge without acting. In December 2021, I co-initiated RiseUp4AbortionRights. I felt I had no choice but to get out and do something. Our first rally was in front of the Supreme Court on January 22, 2022, the forty-ninth anniversary of *Roe v. Wade*. By May of that year, *Politico* published a leaked draft of the majority opinion and the world saw the truth in plain sight, what I had been predicting for half a year. RiseUp was already out in the streets and calling for mass protests. We were active, poised, and ready.

The *Dobbs* Decision: Perceptions and Reality

In June 2022, activists with RiseUp were sleeping in front of the Supreme Court in expectation of the decision coming down. We had to be there when it happened. And it was very good that we were. The cameras from news outlets around the world flashed on the large contingent of anti-abortion activists—Antis. They were orgasmic, of course. There were champagne bottles being opened, joyful outbursts of songs, and chants of "Praise God, Praise Jesus." It was like the Second Coming. On the other side, there were women and girls—hysterical, hugging and supporting each other. In a state of total devastation.

But it was only RiseUp, with our green banners and chants of resistance and struggle—LEGAL ABORTION ON DEMAND NATIONWIDE or FORCED MOTHERHOOD IS FEMALE ENSLAVEMENT—that was making it clear that this decision would not and could not stand. It was a Waterloo moment—a major battle lost. We would fight this for as long as it took. When the decision did come down, the states that had "trigger bans" on their books almost immediately stopped doing abortions. At my clinic, Choices Women's Medical Center, we went from seeing five to eight patients coming from places like Texas and Alabama each month to fifteen a week from Texas alone. For many years, I had been making the point that this struggle was generational. I viewed the wins and losses of court cases as theaters of war, never-ends in themselves. *Dobbs* is no different, only the damage is far more devasting and long-lasting.

Having seen what life was like before abortion was legalized nationally, first in New York and then in Hawaii, Alaska, and Washington State, I do not take anything for granted. You should not either. We must always recognize the complexities, the difficulties, and realities of abortion. Frontline abortion work is a kaleidoscope of issues: religion, love, commitment, sexuality, economics. It is ultimately an encounter with a health care provider (and with the advent and use of the pill, the woman becomes *her own* health care provider). It is not simple or singularly focused, and the work attracts very special kinds of individuals—those who have chosen this work as their mission. While generally unrecognized and underappreciated, I have profound respect for these frontline warriors, from the receptionists to the counselors to the administrators to the doctors.

As far as the large national nonprofit pro-choice organizations, having to serve their funders as well as their mission, there is a type of "political narcissism" that leads many of them to assumptions about the opposition while minimizing the ability to present uncompromising stands. They tend to play public politics safely, preferring instead to incorporate and fundraise off of the radical rhetoric. There is a desire to use reason and logic to win this fight, to compromise with the opposition, to "reason" together. This effort, while admirable, is ultimately futile. You must meet the opposition not in the middle, but where they stand and, hopefully, defeat them for the time being. You cannot stop, though, because they will not stop.

We are living through a powerful, challenging, unprecedented moment, a moment in which a fundamental human and civil right is being ripped away from half the people in this country. The *Dobbs* decision will no doubt reshape the lives of countless women and families for generations to come. We are at war.

It is one thing to struggle for and win a fundamental right. It is quite another to gain one back after a loss. And for those individuals who will succeed me to fight this war and gain back the rights we have lost, I would like to share some of what I've learned—political, ethical, and strategic counsel. These lessons were honed in the fires of experience, challenges, battles, and loss.

I am now seventy-seven years old. I have spent the majority of my conscious life in this struggle. I am often asked how I have been able continue to fight this fight for so long, how I have stood to face the battles and attacks, and how I did not succumb to despair and passivity. In a sense, that famous phrase of Nietzsche's— what doesn't kill you makes you stronger—has been ever-present throughout my life. In time, I came to welcome the battles and challenges that came my way. They became my own special crucible.

I would hope, with this book, to inspire others to do the same, to have courage and fortitude, to look for something beyond their own egos, their "happiness," and their self-gratification. I would like to share the joy, the struggles, and the cost of committing oneself to a cause.

Rising Up to Resist

My politics, passion, and lifelong commitment to Women's Rights and Justice (and what I believe is the foundation of all others) come from the deep understanding that women must retain the moral, biologically "embedded"—and until recently, constitutional—right to decide when and whether or not to be a mother. By definition, this includes the right to legal, safe abortion nationwide.

I founded one of the first abortion clinics in the country in 1971 (abortion was legalized in New York in 1970), two years before *Roe v. Wade*, and in doing so I helped midwife an era in which women came closer to sexual autonomy and freedom than ever before in history. My politics—my "feminism"—came from the ground up, from the experience of being with so many women and girls as they faced the challenge of their choice of abortion.

In the beginning, there was a feminist saying: "Feminism is the theory and abortion is the practice." This was a totally new world. After legalization in 1970, women were lining up around the corners of the big clinics in New York City, one of them doing almost three hundred procedures a day. (It does make one wonder about how many women truly wanted the pregnancies that they were carrying to come to term at that time? And then how many historically were burdened with having children they did not want.) I came to realize that one reason abortion is a positive moral good is because it increases the "wantedness" of each child.

The "issue" of abortion has many faces—lifesaving, life-giving, war, a sin, a choice of victims, a cruel necessity, murder, killing, freedom, power, or just life. The reality of abortion resides in the lived lives of women and girls. "Choice" is sometimes not a choice at all. It is an outcome determined by the economic, physical, sociological, and political factors that surround women and move them toward the only action that allows them to survive at that point in their lives. Survival can sometimes be a woman's act of staying alive, but it can also be her act of refusing to put what will become an impossible burden on her shoulders. Indeed, how can one speak of a choice when currently in this country there is no general support for mothers, no economic security, no comprehensive prenatal care especially for Black and minority women, and millions of us are still without any health care coverage?

Historically, we had won the constitutional right to abortion, and if there were bumps in the road, like the nascent demonstrations outside of clinics that grew into the harassment, the fire bombings, evictions, and invasions, which ultimately escalated to the killing of doctors and clinic workers, "we always had *Roe*" and "they would never take that away."

Well, they could, and they did. The "movement" had made the cardinal mistake of consistently underestimating the power, determination, and relentlessness of the opposition.

The struggle over abortion is not a difference of opinion, nor a religious or theoretical debate. It is, ultimately, a power struggle. Not one Republican or Christian fascist would ever admit to saying that they wanted to have "control" over women's bodies. But banning legal abortion and forcing women to bear children (and children to bear children) against their will is the ultimate means of control—and a form of legal slavery.

The right to legal, safe abortion nationwide is the front line and the bottom line of women's freedom and liberty. Without the right to control their own lives, women's dreams will be deferred or denied, they will bear the children of their rapists, the horizons of their imaginations will be truncated, and their lives will be immensely diminished.

Sir Isaac Newton said, "If I have seen further than others, it is by standing upon the shoulders of giants." My giants are my staff, the women and men who work with me in a constant state of struggle; our patients, the women and girls who come to us and receive the fruits of our collective efforts; and the millions of people in this country fighting in any way they can for this critical and noble cause.

CHAPTER I
THE ROADS TAKEN

I Am Large, I Contain Multitudes

Who am I? To whom? To the world, I am one person; to my daughter, another. To my staff, I am someone else entirely. I can only know these versions of myself through the shared projections of others in a kind of continual feedback loop. But they are so often a distortion.

I am both an intellectual and an activist. Service providers are usually service providers; they are not the ones reading or writing polemics, publishing articles, engaging with the theory. Not only am I a publisher and writer, but an entrepreneur. (The fact that I made money and was comfortable doing so was difficult for many people in the movement to deal with. I am proof that you can be a capitalist with a conscience.) I am not just a heterodox thinker, but a heterodox being. I never did fit into any box. I never wanted to. I never felt comfortable in any of them. Perhaps the only box I will fit into will be the one the bury me in.

I remember being bullied and beaten up by girls when I was in sixth or seventh grade because they didn't like the hairstyle I was wearing. (I think I was channeling George Sand.) I fought back, smashing a lunch plate of mashed potatoes and fried chicken in one of their faces during lunch period. Of course, I was disciplined, but I accepted that as the price to be paid for acting out as a "bad" girl and not just sitting there and taking the abuse.

These nascent ideals are worth everything to me. They have enabled me to survive. They have strengthened my resolve. Real power begins with the power over oneself. Passionate, intense, singular people are often pathologized and derided, but we must embrace our singularity, have psychological courage to go against the wind, and have the power to embrace these attributes and use them for good.

I started my life as an artist—a classical pianist. I read philosophy. I studied criminology and psychology. When I entered the pro-choice arena, I had each of those parts of myself with me and I've carried—and nurtured—them for the last fifty years. I call this "living a mixed life." But like few, I have strived and been gifted by the fates the ability to express many of my selves in reality—and a great number of them through my work with Choices.

I always felt I was destined for a very large stage. And like all children, I was a resistance fighter. From the first time I realized I had the agency, if not the power, to push back against authority, I used it.

I was born in Philadelphia, an only child of an eclectic family. On my mother's side were radicals, musicians, rabbis, and revolutionaries who tried to bomb the Tsar. On my father's side were adventurers and incredibly wealthy entrepreneurs. My father was an autodidact, and we would share poetry and the stories of Sherlock Holmes. My father wanted one thing for me: to be a lady, a good girl who would marry a good man and be "happy."

My mother was the youngest child and the only daughter of six brothers, all of whom she was highly competitive with. She had her own ambitions to go on the stage thwarted (good girls didn't do that) and intensely projected them on me. Because I intimidated her, with my youth and intellectual superiority, she developed her own creative defense. I was always a bad speller, and when I would use a word that my mother did not understand, she would put her hands on her hips and say with a sly grin: "spell it." That was her great equalizer. She loved me, of course, but her love was conditional and narcissistic—she wanted me to be the star she had always wanted to be. I still miss her every day.

As a child between these two adults, I felt unknown, unseen, and misunderstood. I had no role models to speak of. The prevailing idea was that I could aspire to be a nurse or a teacher because that way I would have a job to fall back on if my husband were to die or leave me.

I was rebellious by nature. When I wanted to look out a window in a classroom, I got up and looked. Once, when I had to lie quietly on a blanket for rest period, I decided I wanted to visit the other kids. So I did. As punishment for this crime, they put me in the coat closet where I had to sit quietly, looking at animal stickers. (I still remember that damn bunny I had to stare at for what seemed like hours.) Another time, I was caught changing a report card grade for behavior, and I quickly made up a story about how my mother was ill and near death to get out of it. (It didn't work.)

The boundaries I pushed back against had more to do with my insistent curiosity and constant motion than my gender. I never had the impression that I was held back or down because I was a girl. Rather, it was because my parents and teachers had difficulty controlling me.

After we moved from Philadelphia to Kew Gardens in Queens, New York, I started to haunt the library near my home. I remember walking in and being surrounded by a sense of sacredness. I was drawn to the left-hand side, where under a large sign— BIOGRAPHIES—I happened upon a book about Elizabeth the First of England. With that discovery, my entire interior world changed. Totally bereft of heroic female narratives and role models up until that point, I can only compare the experience to an epiphany.

Elizabeth, I read, went from a prison to a palace and ascended the throne at twenty-five years old. Here was a woman who ruled alone for forty-five years, in which time she moved her small bankrupt island country into the beginnings of an empire. Elizabeth had absolute power. Although there was a functioning parliament, she had the right to disband it at will.

Elizabeth was also a survivor. Born to Henry VIII and Anne Boleyn, her mother was beheaded when Elizabeth was three years old in a judicial murder so that Henry could marry his third wife and hopefully produce his longed-for male heir. Elizabeth was officially declared a bastard and lost her place in the succession, was groomed and sexually abused when she was thirteen, and was accused of organizing a plot against her half-sister Bloody Mary I, who was on the throne at the time. She was sent to the Tower and was inches away from losing her head. But she didn't.

Instead, through her own astute political ability and laser focus, she survived to mount the throne at twenty-five. She never married—absolute anathema in the sixteenth century, particularly for a female monarch—and she ruled alone. Elizabeth created a fantastic persona—a combination of the goddess Diana and the Virgin Mary (she was, indeed, known as the Virgin Queen because never wed and never bore children)—and was a marvelous public relations person and spin doctor. She helped create the "Good Queen Bess" icon, even though she could be as ruthless and cruel as any one of her contemporaries. And she was brilliant, a scholar who spoke five languages and could debate in Latin. She was a great orator and a deep thinker. She may have been psychologically damaged, but she used her wounds as bullets and shields. She fought the might of Spain and vanquished the Spanish Armada.

It was as if I were reading about an alien. A woman, yes, but one who had the largest stage and within the boundaries and realities of her time created a unique self—a mythological androgynous self, unique not only for her time but all time. There were rumors that she was a man because it was so hard to believe that a woman could rule alone.

An only child, I spent hours in my room alone reading and acting out fantasies of heroines of the past. I acted out the beheading of Mary Queen of Scots as well as Elizabeth's speech to her troops at Tilbury as the Armada approached: "I have the heart and stomach of a king, and a King of England, too." I was Joan of Arc, perpetually being burned at the stake. All my games were political, as Indira Gandhi said.

From Music to Activism: Songs of Myself

Classical music was a major part of my mother's family. My first cousin, Marilyn—the only real-life role model I had—was a violin prodigy who played Carnegie Hall at eleven years old. Her three siblings, and my uncle and aunt, were also serious musicians. However, my cousin was the star of the family, and her concerts and accomplishments were always front and center at family gatherings. A natural competitiveness with Marilyn and my love of music led me to begin studying the piano when I was ten. As it happened, I also was extremely gifted in music, and until I was twenty-one, I trained to be a concert pianist. When I graduated from the High School of Music and Art, I decided not to go to college and to study music in Paris.

Through classical music I learned about sex and gender. I remember my first teacher telling me, when I wanted to play Liszt's "Mephisto Waltz," that "girls usually don't play that, dear. I would suggest Mozart." There was also the physical differentiation. I had small hands and some of Chopin and a great deal of Liszt required a hand that could stretch two octaves. Even though I would spend hours trying to stretch the space between my fingers, much of that spectacular repertoire would remain impossible for me. Nevertheless, I became an excellent pianist.

While studying abroad in Paris, I learned my father was ill in the hospital and I immediately returned home. Just like that, my bohemian artistic life was finished, and I landed back in bourgeois Queens where I immediately entered my first existential crisis. I was still practicing the piano daily, but in reality, it became clear to me that I did not, in fact, want to be a concert artist. The life was far too hermetic: five to six hours of practice each day. Music would have to be my *entire* life, and music, as they say, is a cruel mistress.

Rather than the ultimate vehicle for self-expression, music began to seem like a kind of prison. Like Kafka's "bird in search of a cage," I knew I needed to land somewhere. But where? And doing what? I read voraciously, painted a bit, and signed up for courses at the Art Students' League. I took some acting classes at the Herbert Bergdorf Studio. Generally, however, I felt totally unmoored. I landed some part-time jobs, but who was I, really—truly—without the piano? Through a family friend, a visiting professor at NYU, I would find a way out of that life and into another. He recognized my insatiable intellectual curiosity and recommended that I apply.

I had been there for almost a year when my father died. As a result of his death, I could not afford the tuition at NYU and transferred to Queens College. I worked three part-time jobs to support myself and graduated as a member of Phi Beta Kappa. From there, I went to the CUNY Graduate Center for my doctoral work in social psychology.

One of the jobs I had around this time was working as a medical assistant for a physician, Dr. Martin Gold, in his private office. Dr. Gold would later become my husband and my partner in founding Flushing Women's Medical Center in 1971, one of the first legal abortion clinics in the country. Initially conceived as an outpatient abortion facility for the Health Insurance Plan (HIP) and founded with the guidance of Dr. Alan Guttmacher (the father of Planned Parenthood), this was where I found my calling. I still remember my first patient. Helen.

Helen came from New Jersey because, in 1971, abortion remained illegal in New Jersey and most of the country until the *Roe* ruling in 1973. She came in with her husband and one of her three children. I remember that she was visibly shaking with anxiety. Dr. Gold said to me, "Go in and talk to her." I was nervous, too. No one had trained me. Legal abortion was an uncharted course full of morality, theology, philosophy, and politics—all topics I'd studied—but I had no experience in dealing directly with the abortion "patient" herself. No one did.

I thought to myself, *What do I say? What do I do?* The intellectual giants of psychology came into my mind, but Freud and Jung had nothing to say about dealing with the ultimate questions of existence (the woman's and the fetus's) in a medical setting. I went into the room, sat down, and told her up front that this was the first time I had done this.

"We are pioneers in this new world of legal abortion," I said. "I'm going to talk to you about what the procedure involves and the physical, emotional, and psychological aspects of it. But let me first assure you that you are not going to die. You are in a safe professional medical space now."

In the early days, abortion meant death or potentially life-altering complications. Indeed, the very first time I heard about an abortion was when I was ten years old. I overheard my parents whispering about a Philadelphia physician whose patient died when he was performing an illegal abortion and to cover it up, the doctor cut the woman up and put her remains down the drain. Abortion, for many people, brought to mind images of death and disfigurement. People had been raised on movies with horrid and realistic illegal abortion scenes where women died or were butchered. (Or they lived, only to be punished by society and made an example of.)

Helen told me it was impossible to have another child, that her family would be financially broken and that she psychologically was unable to care for one more. I spoke with her husband, who was extremely supportive. At that time, we did not have the space or equipment for general anesthesia, which for many years was the reality in most clinics around the country. I told her the pain would be similar to bad period cramps and tried to reassure her. "I will stay with you," I said. I remember gently touching her hair and leaning in close and speaking softly into her ear, telling her she was making the right choice and that everything would be okay. During the procedure, she was squeezing my hand so tightly I had to take off my ring. I told her to breathe in, breathe out, breathe in, breathe out. I breathed, too, matching my rhythm with hers.

After it was over, I had the profound experience of being in the recovery room with her as she expressed her relief and gratitude for just being alive and not pregnant. It was another epiphany: This is not a career; this is not a job. This is a mission.

And there was always another—another woman or little girl, another face, another set of eyes wide open with fear. There was, in those early days, so much fear. But the ability to look in these women's eyes and say, "It's over. You're not pregnant anymore," was and *is* a gift to them and to me. In that moment, their life is being given back to them. The patient is so vulnerable. They are lying on the GYN table, their legs placed in the stirrups, spread in that primal position. Very quickly, I learned the power of opening myself up to them—of "active loving."

Many of the patients had never been listened to—alone—for a serious conversation in a professional setting. I treated them with dignity, respect, and compassion. I never shared my judgments about their choices with them, nor did I move them toward one decision or another. I have always believed that we must separate the chooser from the choice. While I will not always agree with *why* someone is having an abortion, I profoundly believe it must be the woman who chooses.

After years of hearing what women had gone through, I had to develop a protective veil. I could not take into myself all the life stories, all the trauma, all the time. But I could lower it just for the time it took to connect and engage with the women. Since I called my medical center Choices ("Creative Health Organization for Information Counseling and Educational Services"), after a few years I began a prenatal program so I could really "operationalize" that word.

Working with the women in those years was deeply meaningful. But there was so much else to manage. I had to put an entire system together, to create roles and functions, hire and fire staff, deal with vendors, calculate the deductions for payroll, get involved with banking—all of which required me to be creative, pragmatic, and disciplined. After I was unionized by 1199, I was negotiating union contracts and dealing with the politically explosive decision of the employees voting to leave the union, all by the age of twenty-seven. I was simultaneously creating and actualizing my vision of a unique feminist medical center.

It was work that would lead me deep into the *politics* of abortion. I remember it distinctly—the point in time when I became political: It was summer, 1976. Monotonic radio voices intruded while I stayed in bed longer than usual. Something about Henry Hyde and abortion. Now I was all ears. Republican congressman Henry Hyde had succeeded in passing legislation that would effectively eliminate the right of women on Medicaid to have an abortion. Hyde said, "If we can't save all the babies, then at least we can save the babies of the poor." His answer was to cut off Medicaid funding for the poorest women in the country. I found this egregious and extraordinarily discriminatory. These were the young women, Black women, minority women, struggling women that I saw every day at Choices.

Hearing that news, I was filled with an intense self-awareness, coupled with a strong feeling of fate. I instinctively knew that my life was irrevocably changed. It was as if some imaginary line had been drawn separating my beginnings from what ultimately would become the "real stuff"—my true life's work.

By 1976, I had already been immersed for five years in the reality of abortion: women and women's lives! But now it was time to talk about it, to fight for it. Those women from whom Henry Hyde would callously cut off abortion rights were my women, my patients—people I lived with every day. These women were what Choices was all about. I thought of Martin Niemöller's famous words:

First they came for the socialists, and I did not speak out—because I was not a socialist. Then they came for the trade unionists, and I did not speak out—because I was not a trade unionist. Then they came for the Jews, and I did not speak out—because I was not a Jew. Then they came for me—and there was no one left to speak for me.

When the Hyde Amendment passed, I saw clearly the truth of this situation, which was that eventually they would come for all of us. This inspired my first political act, which was to write a one-page polemic, print out hundreds of copies, and go into the halls of Queens College (my alma mater) to distribute them. I called it a "Women's Rights State of Emergency."

Aside from handing them out to students outside, I knocked on classroom doors and asked professors if I could come in to address their classes. Something needed to be done, I told them. Students reacted with both metaphorical and physical shoulder shrugs, while some said, "If I need to, I will be able to get one."

These were middle-class white kids I was speaking to. There was no concern at all. No caring. That's when I really began to view the abortion issue through the lenses of race and class.

Of course the legislation went through handily, regardless of my small protest, but in that moment, I made the transition from the personal to the political, from the world of singular experience to the broader, more demanding and dangerous one of social and political activism.

As part of my work with patients, I also began to develop a philosophy drawn from the many writers, philosophers, and historical role models in my life up to that point. Working with patients became a powerful way to synthesize these deeply felt personas and ideas and put them into practice on the only stage I had: my clinic.

In the first or second year of Flushing Women's, for example, a couple of the nursing staff requested that they not have to wear white coats. They felt the patients would be more comfortable and less anxious if the staff wore dark scrubs and their own sweatshirts. Coming from a social psychological background, I decided to test that hypothesis and give the patients a questionnaire asking them. Almost 98 percent preferred the white coats because they felt them to be more "professional." A person in a white coat was considered more "trustworthy." This was shortly after abortion was legalized in New York and images of the back alleys, bloody coat hangers, and dead bodies were still very much on everyone's mind.

But I wanted to be a stellar leader, one that makes informed decisions, so I collected data from the people who would be most affected. I was responsible for my own small country, and I was in charge, but I was open minded. And the decisions that I made were important; they affected women's lives. I listened carefully to all opinions, but the decisions were mine because the responsibility was mine. It was my head on the block.

My reading of history and the great actors of history had a large influence on me, especially in those early years. The French Revolution was ripe with role models and characters I could relate to. Camille Desmoulins, for example, gave the call to arms—"To arms! Let us all wear green cockades, the color of hope"—that made the crowd in Paris rise up on July 12, 1789, and storm the Bastille two days later. He was arrested and guillotined in April 1794. (It is interesting to note that green has a long history as the color of revolutionary struggle, a history that includes Riseup4abortionrights.)

There was Charlotte Corday, from whose "oversoul" I descended, according to a reading by a famous psychic. Corday was a committed Girondist who at only twenty-six years old assassinated the leading radical Jacobian Jean-Paul Marat as he lay in his bathtub writing yet another polemic calling for more heads to roll. (Andre Marie de Chenier wrote the "Ode to Marie-Anne-Charlotte-Corday" as he watched her in the tumbrel going to the guillotine in a light rain, her head held high.)

I looked to Olympe de Gouges, the political activist and playwright who wrote, "Woman is born free and lives equal to man in her rights. Social distinctions can be based only on the common utility." In her "Declaration of the Rights of Woman and of the Female Citizen," she challenged the notion and practice of male authority and male-female inequality. "Women have the right to mount the scaffold," she wrote. "They should likewise have the right to mount the rostrum." She was also a passionate abolitionist. She, too, was guillotined.

There were, of course, Elizabeth I and her nemesis Mary Queen of Scots, Joan of Arc and, later, Sophie Scholl—the great student resister to Hitler's Nazi regime. So many of these singular individuals ended up on the scaffold or the stake. At times I, too, have felt as though I have been on a slow burn for years. In awe of these women who died such noble deaths under such horrific circumstances, I often tried to imagine how I would react on a scaffold.

My extant role model and political mentor was Bella Abzug— "Battling Bella"—whom I first heard giving a passionate antiwar speech in the crowded ballroom of the Statler Hilton for the First Women's Health Forum, which I helped organize. The hairs on the back of my neck stood up as she spoke. *That's it*, I thought. *That's what I want to be doing.* I will never forget a rally I organized in a major snowstorm on one anniversary of *Roe v. Wade*. After I had made my speech, I went back to stand next to her.

"Good job, kid," she said in her gruff manner. I can still hear the words all these years later. Another lesson I learned from those who came before me: young women, rather than minimizing the lessons of the past, or of history itself, should think deeply about learning from our foremothers. If we choose or are chosen to be leaders, we must also learn to follow.

CHAPTER 2
ROE V. WADE AND CHOICES

Supply and Demand: Back-Alley Abortions and the Alternatives

When abortion is legal, a woman can feel confident and comfortable going to their physician, OB-GYN, or directly into a clinic and saying, "I want to terminate my pregnancy." Since abortion is one of the safest outpatient procedures, there is minimal risk. According to a 2012 study, "the risk of death associated with childbirth is approximately 14 times higher than that with abortion."[2] (Not long ago, male physicians worked on cadavers in hospitals and then went immediately into the operating room to deliver a baby without washing their hands. Women would prepare their wills prior to going into labor.)

Conversely, when abortion is illegal, the provider will be taking a major risk—essentially engaging in criminal activity. (The recent disciplinary action against a doctor in Indiana for treating a ten-year-old rape victim is but a prelude of what is to come.)[3] Likewise, if many of the current Republican initiatives manage to pass, women in some states in this country will face the death penalty for abortion. Lest one think this is mere hyperbole, as reported by the *Ohio Capital Journal*, "an all-male panel of anti-abortion religious leaders

---

2 Elizabeth G. Raymond and David A. Grimes, "The comparative safety of legal induced abortion and childbirth in the United States," *Obstet. Gynecol*, February 2012.
3 Kim Bellware and Dan Rosenzweig-Ziff, "Indiana Board Fines Doctor for Discussing Rape Victim's Abortion," *Washington Post*, May 25, 2023, https://www.washingtonpost.com/nation/2023/05/25/caitlin-bernard-indiana-abortion-rape-victim/.

from around the country" met in Georgia in July 2023 "to discuss the strategies that should be used to end abortion in every state at any stage of pregnancy, without exceptions for rape and incest, and with criminal punishment for the pregnant person in line with existing criminal penalties for murder, which includes the death penalty."[4]

Women who are unable to access a doctor for a surgical abortion or for the "pill" have two choices—if one can even consider this a choice. They can do nothing and become "breeders"—slaves to the State who will carry and birth children they do not want and probably cannot care for, which will upend their lives and their families. Or they can resort to age-old self-abortion techniques and hope they live through it.

Over the centuries, women have tried any number of home remedies to induce a miscarriage. They will go into freezing and then hot water. They will throw themselves down stairs. They will use lye. They will use a hanger. Historically, many of these women ended up becoming septic and dying. My late husband, Dr. Martin Gold, had done his residency at Bellevue hospital and used to talk to me about the "midnight express," which was what they called it when women would come in bleeding from a botched self-abortion attempt. The hospital would take them in, diagnose them as a miscarriage, and do a dilation and curettage procedure, which was basically an abortion.

Bill Baird (known as the "father of the abortion movement") decided to spend his life and career in birth control and abortion advocacy after witnessing the death of a woman from a failed coathanger abortion.[5] She was the mother of nine children, and she

---

4 Kelcie Moseley-Morris, "Male Anti-abortion Religious Leaders Mull Murder Charges For Pregnant People at National Event," *Ohio Capital Journal*, July 25, 2023, https://ohiocapitaljournal.com/2023/07/25/male-anti-abortion-religious-leaders-mull-murder-charges-for-pregnant-people-at-national-event/.

5 After giving a condom and contraceptive foam to a female college student at a Boston University in 1967, Baird—a speaker and reproductive rights advocate—was arrested under Massachusetts's "Crimes Against Chastity, Decency, Morality and Good Order" law, which prohibited providing contraceptives to unmarried persons. He was convicted and sentenced to three months in jail. He appealed his conviction and fought for five years until a 1972 Supreme Court decision, *Eisenstadt v. Baird*, finally legalized birth control for all Americans.

died bleeding in his arms. Baird's epiphany, like mine, was forged in blood.

Of course, there were always women who had the money and connections to go to doctors who had the courage and backup to do abortions—for a high price. (Before abortion was legalized, if you were fortunate enough, you might have also been connected to referral services like Jane,[6] an underground abortion network and feminist referral center whose volunteers routinely risked going to jail for the greater good, or the Clergy Consultation Center, which consisted of a group of twenty-one Protestant ministers and Jewish rabbis who began working together out of the Judson Memorial Church in New York City. The group would grow to incorporate chapters in thirty-eight states with some three thousand clergy as members, and by the time of the *Roe v. Wade* decision in 1973, it is estimated that the Clergy Consultation service had nationally referred at least 450,000 people for safe abortions from licensed medical professionals.) For most women, however, the horror, fear, diminishment, and shame of having to resort to awful solutions— usually alone—to *try* to terminate a pregnancy is not something one has to experience firsthand to understand. One needs only the smallest amount of imaginative empathy to recognize the dreadfulness of such a situation.

After *Roe*, everything changed. Patients no longer had to travel to the few states that had legalized abortion and could access services much closer to where they lived. In New York, there were a couple of clinics that had prepared for this and were performing two to three hundred abortions a day in eight operating rooms.

An example of why hospitals were not the appropriate venue for the volume of abortions required, nor the supportive environment, particularly in the second trimester, was the practice of

---

6 The Jane Collective, officially known as the Abortion Counseling Service of Women's Liberation, was a covert Chicago-based referral and abortion service that operated from 1969 to 1972. The group is estimated to have performed eleven thousand abortions, many of which were done by non-medical members of the group who had learned how to carry out surgical abortions. No Jane clients were known to have died from the procedure.

"saline abortions." Before the practice of Dilation & Evacuation (D&Es) (which have been continually attacked as "partial birth abortions"), hospitals would do "saline abortions," in which the doctor would put saline into the uterus and the patient would go into labor and deliver a dead fetus. This procedure could only be done on patients who were sixteen weeks or larger. So, if a patient came into Choices and was fourteen weeks pregnant (because we were not doing second-trimester procedures in clinics), they would have to wait until they were sixteen weeks, depending on a sonographic reading. Then they could go into the hospital for a second-trimester procedure.

Hospitals would then put these women into the labor and delivery rooms with other patients who were delivering live babies. Most of the nurses didn't want to work with them. Most of the other patients didn't want to deal with them. The inability of hospitals to handle all the attending issues surrounding abortion is one of the main reasons freestanding clinics became so critical to the provision of these services.

Founding Choices

In large part, those early years saw great bursts of insight and creativity. Clinics opened in the more urban and progressive areas like Los Angeles and San Francisco, but also in the South and across the Bible Belt. It was such a vibrant era, percolating with new concepts, where feminist ideas and philosophy could actually be put into practice. When I founded Choices in 1971,[7] women's health as a discipline, as a practice, and as a vision simply did not exist. Legal abortion brought abortion out of the back alleys and women's health care out of the closet. It radicalized the status of women in society and revolutionized their relationship with the health care establishment.

---

7 Originally called Flushing Women's Medical Center, I changed it to Choices when I moved out of the basement of the HIP group to my own space in the Lefrak building on Queens Blvd.

The first few years after *Roe* were the salad days. Clinics became feminist planets. Where else could a twenty-six-year-old have the authority to hire and fire doctors and staff, develop modalities for counseling patients, and create new protocols for interactions with staff? This was a brave and radical new world; and it really felt like it was *ours*. It was a heady time—where one woman's unique-yet-collective experience of an unplanned and unwanted pregnancy intersected with a new feminist politic of freedom and responsibility. We inhabited a place where we made women's lives matter; a time when feminism resonated with risk and spoke of struggle rather than privilege. There were so many firsts.

For the first time, women were in control of patient referrals and clinics, while physicians were brought down from their godlike pedestals to function as employees of medical centers that were, at least in the early days, often owned or run by feminists. At Choices, counseling sessions were done by young feminist activists whom I trained in abortion issues. The training included discussions about sexuality, religion, love, psychology, and death, which augmented the technical medical explanations of the procedure. As a result, the traditional medical bifurcation of mind/body was exploded by operationally integrating politics, psychology, and clinical treatment. In those early days, I treated many women whose unwanted pregnancies stemmed from their victimization by the medical establishment (their gynecologists). I coined the term "iatrogenic pregnancies" to describe unplanned pregnancies due to ignorance, misinformation, prejudice, or the withholding of accurate information by their doctors.

I started building the clinic as a neophyte, but, as I wrote in my memoir, *Intimate Wars*, over the next several years, I became more and more connected to the work, the women, and from there, to radical political activism.

I wrote:

> After a few years of directing Flushing Women's [Medical Center], my days at the clinic had begun to feel a little more

routine. By then, we were seeing fifty women a week, and at that time I was still counseling most of them.

I can't remember how many hands I held, how many heads I caressed, how many times I whispered into how many ears, "It will be all right, just breathe slowly." I saw so much vulnerability: legs spread wide apart; the physician crouched between Black, White, heavy, thin, but always trembling, thighs; the tube sucking the fetal life from their bodies.

"It'll be over soon, just take one more deep breath"—the last thrust and pull of the catheter—then the gurgle that signaled the end of the abortion. Gynecologists called it the "uterine cry." Over and over again, I witnessed women's invariable relief after their abortion that they were not dead, that God did not strike them down by lightning, that they could walk out of this place not pregnant anymore: that their lives had been given back to them.

It was the kind of born-again experience that often resulted in promises: I will never do this again. I will always make him wear condoms. I will be more careful next time.

It was the very young girls that moved me most. I felt so much rage against the males who impregnated each child—was it her father, her brother, some young boy with no thought for the consequences? The girls, the women, were duly punished for their part of the sex act. But for the boy or man there was no censure, never was.

At times I was filled with a kind of bitter resignation. I knew that I might see each again soon. So many of them were barely more than babies themselves when pregnancy came, unplanned and unwanted. They were innocent and often ignorant, didn't believe they were pregnant until it was too late to deny it, too afraid to ask for help at first. "Maybe it'll go away," they reasoned.

I spent hours counseling husbands, lovers, sisters, and mothers whose fury at their daughters' betrayal needed a kind of salve I couldn't give. "Let her get local anesthesia," they said. "Let her really feel the pain so she knows never to do it again." The daughters' heads lay on my shoulder as I sat on their beds, wiping tears of relief or regret or both, whispering comfort, giving absolution, channeling rage, sharing life.

"I would want to keep this pregnancy, if only…" I learned that it is in the "if only" that the reality of abortion resides. It's there in the vast expanse of a lived life—the sum of experience, the pull of attachment, the pain of ambivalence. "If only" is a theme with thousands of variations.

If only I wasn't fourteen.

If only I was married.

If only my husband had another job.

If only I didn't give birth to a baby six months ago.

If only I didn't just get accepted to college.

If only I didn't have such difficult pregnancies.

If only I wasn't in this lousy marriage.

If only I wasn't forty-two.

If only my boyfriend wasn't on drugs.

If only I wasn't on drugs.

If only . . .

I bore witness to each woman's knowledge of holding the power to decide whether or not to allow the potential life within her to come to term.

The act of abortion positions women at their most powerful, and that is why it is so strongly opposed by many in society. Historically viewed and conditioned to be passive, dependent creatures, victims of biological circumstance, women assume the power over life and death with the choice of abortion, an awkward mantle for many. They fall prey to the assumption—the myth—that women should not be trusted with this ultimate power.

What we achieved in the years after *Roe* changed the lives of women across the country. We opened the doors for women to access an array of health services. We reduced the number of unintended pregnancies, which led to lower rates of depression, suicide, and physical abuse. We allowed women to enter the workforce in numbers previously unseen. We empowered women to pursue careers that would have been otherwise completely inaccessible. And we advanced the field of safe abortions and women's health care, reducing the associated risks for millions of women.[8]

The positive societal impact of these and other achievements, which came as a direct result of *Roe v. Wade*, cannot be overstated. Personally, being so involved and present at the birth of this new feminist world, I was able to express and actualize almost all my personality, skills, and creative impulses. In the early 1970s, when many minority and special interest groups were exploring their own histories and asserting their rights, the acknowledgment of patients as a class—intrinsically holding rights and responsibilities—seemed an appropriate analytical and political vehicle for what I clinically experienced as a general victimization of women (patients) by a generally male medical establishment.

Many standard medical practices of the day were sexist, invasive, and paternalistic. In response, I developed many patient-centered tenets and practices and implemented them at Choices, which have since become standards of female and feminist health care. This was especially true in the area of reproductive issues where trust, ignorance, fear, and dependency resulted in a myriad of problems such as unnecessary mastectomies, hysterectomies, dangerous IUDs, experimental hormonal therapies, and iatrogenic pregnancies. Story after story, woman after woman, come to mind.

"My doctor told me to go off the pill to give my body a rest. He never said we had to use anything else."

"My doctor didn't believe in sterilizing me because he said I wasn't old enough and didn't have enough children."

"My doctor said he gave all his women IUDs."

"My doctor said he didn't have to refit my diaphragm after my last abortion."

"My doctor told me I could use foam."

---

8 "Advising the Nation After Roe v. Wade: Cascading Impacts on Women's Health, Family Well-Being, and Society," National Academies, October 14, 2022, https://www .nationalacademies.org/news/2022/10/advising-the-nation-after-roe-v-wade-cascading -impacts-on-womens-health-family-well-being-and-society.

Patient Power

I realized early on that female patients constituted an oppressed class in relation to their physicians. Understanding that "power concedes nothing without demand," I developed at Choices the philosophy of "Patient Power," which taught that patients had rights that included informed consent to treatment, second opinions, the ability to review their medical records, and access to alternative treatment options.

On the other hand, patients were responsible for engaging honestly and directly with providers and educating themselves about their own bodies. This construct was first published in 1975 in the *Journal of the International Academy of Preventive Medicine*. I made the case that it was the woman in the family who made the decisions about who and when someone went to the doctor. Women were the major consumers of health care, and as such should have a voice and role in determining treatments, schedules, and referrals.

The kernel of Patient Power was to empower patients as a class with a class consciousness. This thinking has slowly expanded throughout many consumer and health movements in this country. The women's health care movement has played a major role by concentrating and focusing much of its energies on educating a traditionally ignorant and passive population—women patients. This was the Reformation! For the first time, women's health information was being written by women; doctors, mainly male doctors, were no longer in complete control of the narratives; and women could educate themselves with seminal—or *ovular*, perhaps— works like *Our Bodies, Ourselves*. This was Patient Power at its height! (The advent of the internet and the plethora of information available has changed this radically. Now, patients come "armed" with their own research and facts.)

My theory of Patient Power led to now-standard practices, such as having another staff member in the room with a male doctor and patient at all times and developing the concept of informed consent; having other women counselors rather than doctors provide emotional support and answer patients' questions during abortions; and using patients' abortion-based clinic visits as a gateway to provide sexual health education as well as counseling on birth control options. I urged women to question their doctor about everything from their training and background to the reason for prescribing certain medications. My work was noted by Francis X. Clines in *The New York Times* as "making women feel powerful."

In November 1974, I initiated and moderated New York City's first Women's Health Forum, sponsored by the Health Insurance Plan of New York, with Barbara Ehrenreich and Congresswoman Bella Abzug giving the keynote speeches. In 1975, I helped develop and introduce a program to diagnose women with breast cancer in an outpatient center. The program, known as STOP (Second Treatment Option Program), was pathbreaking. Prior to its inception, women were not consulted regarding their diagnosis or treatment options. Previously, doctors had simply removed the breast of any woman whose biopsy came back positive while she was still anesthetized and *on the operating table*—that is, before she had the opportunity to learn about her options or make decisions.

Finding this an egregious exercise of medical power and learning that Queens had some of the highest rates of breast cancer in the country, I knew I had to act. I reached out to Dr. Gene Thiessen, founder of Share (Self-Help Action & Rap Experience), and together we developed the first outpatient breast cancer diagnostic and treatment program. In 1976, I founded and became the first president of the National Abortion Federation (NAF). I remember at one of the first meetings when we were discussing what the mission of the organization should be, someone suggested, "to further the interests of abortion facilities." I didn't know anyone there and no one knew me, but I knew what the mission of the organization should be. So I got up and said, "No, the mission must be to further the interests of *women and patients*."

There was a point where I felt that legalizing abortion had elevated the status of women as patients. I called it the Medical

ERA for women because for the first time it was required that a medical procedure was to be done by the *physician in consultation* with the woman. The law had unedified physicians and required them to have the educated consent of the patient before making the decision to perform a surgical procedure (abortion). I viewed this as a triumph of Patient Power.

Many radical feminists at the time of *Roe v. Wade* thought and continue to think that *Roe v. Wade* was too much of a compromise. "Why should doctors be involved at all in the decision?" they reasoned. There is also a long history of some radical feminists promoting "menstrual extraction," which was a method developed by Carol Downer and Lorraine Rothman as an inexpensive women-controlled alternative to physician abortion and performed without a positive pregnancy test. As the Pill becomes less and less available—and there are now twenty-three million women who have absolutely no access to legal safe surgical abortions—these self-help methods will be revisited. However, the (theoretical) purity of that thinking was drowned out by the radical nature of how *Roe* would change all women's lives.

CHAPTER 3
A WOMEN'S RIGHTS STATE OF EMERGENCY

A Real War with Real Casualties

After *Roe*, any sense of victory was short-lived because the struggle for abortion rights always was, and always will be, a war. Nearly *thirty-five years ago, and twenty-seven years after Roe,* I wrote the following explanation in *On the Issues* for why the struggle for reproductive rights was a real war with real casualties:

> Because doctors and health care workers are being shot dead in their clinics.
>
> Because abortion is unavailable to many millions of American, and some patients must still risk their lives to have one.
>
> Because we are held hostage to the political agendas that disallow even the smallest move forward.
>
> Because of continuing racial and class divisions that block collective action among women.
>
> Because women who have abortions continue to deny the fact that they did.
>
> I once attended a national meeting of providers who reacted to my description of abortion as a fundamental civil right as "not sellable to the American public"—promulgating a view of abortion as "tragic but necessary," the pro-choice movement has succeeded in remaining in an apologetic and reactive position. Instead of an aggressive visionary strategy we are continually

defending things that should require no defense—women's lives and freedom. We are *now* in the ultimate defensive position—defending this state by state as the casualties mount!

We must reclaim and honor our history. We must remember the women who, alone and in pain, lost their lives for their right to choose.

We must throw off our personal shrouds of shame and tell the stories of our mothers and grandmothers, and ourselves.

We must close the split between the strategists and national leaders of the pro-choice movement and its foot soldiers, the women who have actually had abortions and the providers who make them possible. Together, we must reposition and redefine legal abortion as an integral core of women's health and as the necessary condition for women's freedom.

Nothing stops abortion—no law, no government, no religious authority. Making abortion illegal only makes it dangerous and deadly.

The movement must speak with a unified voice that articulates a shared vision. Abortion and reproductive freedom are fundamental human rights, not to be abridged by any entity. We must actively strategize, not only for the next skirmish or the next battle, but for the coming twenty-five years—to ensure that our daughters and granddaughters do not have to fight the same war.

We must work to regain lost allies (the American Medical Association voted to uphold the ban on "partial birth" abortion). We must move in powerful coalition with other progressive movements—gays and lesbians, civil rights organizations, environmental activists, labor—and demand that the leadership of these movements actively support reproductive freedom.

We must expose the fifth column within our own ranks, feminists who are "pro-choice" but handle their personal discomfort with abortion by naming it a "tragedy" and thus making it more difficult for others to choose freely.

We must expand the definition of pro-choice to include those women living with racism and poverty for whom the right to reproductive freedom means the right to bear children with adequate financial and medical support.

We must reach out to the young women who live a feminism of entitlement rather than struggle, and do not understand that freedom requires constant vigilance.

We must be militant when necessary and be ready to sacrifice more than freedom for the cause.

We must creatively develop new legal theories that further secure the constitutional basis of reproductive freedom.

Finally, we must be able to speak the truth to ourselves by answering the question, "Is it a woman's right to choose or is it killing?" by saying yes—to both—and taking full responsibility for that profound and powerful truth. The answer to this philosophical challenge is within the realpolitik of each woman's heart.

Twenty-seven years and who's counting? I'm counting—counting the days and years and decades until all women will live in a world where reproductive freedom is a fundamental human right and no one will ever again die for her right to choose.

It has now been fifty-two years and I am still counting. A war doesn't stop simply because a battle has been won. After we won that right, many of the activists put their feet up on the desk and said, "We have *Roe v. Wade*. We won. Now let's stop focusing so much on abortion." I don't believe you win these kinds of struggles. They are, as I've said, generational struggles. There will always be opposition, which will require constant vigilance. In our case, the movement failed to take seriously what was happening with the opposition, their long-term strategy and ultimate goal. Which leads us, once again, to *Dobbs*.

"Settled" Law

Dobbs v. Jackson Women's Health Organization: This is where *Roe* ends and where we must begin—again. What does it mean for all of us? What does it mean for women, for families, for children, for the stress on the health care system, for providers, for clinics, for the promise of this country? A decision that strips a fundamental civil and human right from more than half the population will inevitably and dangerously metastasize to every area of society.

Dobbs didn't appear like a thunderbolt in the sky. The certainty of it was neither a surprise nor a major shock—not, at least, if you lived in or followed this particular "theater of war," as I did. I knew it was coming. I knew it was going to be argued before the Supreme Court and I knew that it was going to be decided in June. I knew, too, how it would be decided. Each and every decision that led to *Dobbs* had been on my personal radar. After all, I had been following the opposition closely for decades. When Trump and the Republicans managed to appoint three conservative Catholic Supreme Court justices, there was a collective insight of sorts: "My god, now they have the votes. They can actually do it." But there were *still so many others* saying: "They can't do it. They won't do it. They'll never do it."

The prevailing wisdom was not that *Roe* would not be overturned, but that it *could not* be overturned. It was "settled law." The confidence in the system and in the idea of "settled law" led to an imaginary Maginot Line that, presumably, no one would cross. This confidence was borne out of a misunderstanding of the opposition. But from the beginning, the Antis have been focused on one goal: overturning *Roe*. Overturning *Roe* is but the first major step toward the ultimate goal of banning abortion nationwide and elevating the legal status of the fetus to that of a person. They have changed strategies according to the political contexts in which they've had to work, and they have learned to pivot on a dime.

"You think we don't care about women?" the Antis ask before offering up studies that show how many women "regret" their abortions and studies that show how abortion causes breast cancer and infertility. The *fact* is abortion is an extremely safe procedure with a safety record of over 99 percent. As a matter of fact, studies have found that there is a greater chance of complications from getting your wisdom teeth removed than from having an abortion. Now, you think the pills will save you? Watch the plethora of legislative and legal attempts to ban the distribution and use of them.

First, the Antis harassed people outside of clinics, then they attacked clinics and providers—but the objective never changed. The strategy would change depending on who was in the White House. There have been more killings and more violence with Democrats in power, for example, than with Republicans. But the opposition have shown themselves to be exceedingly flexible, vigilant, and strategic. I've always said that I admire their creativity and it is true. I respect their persistence, their consistency, their very real ability to move according to their prime directive. We never took them seriously enough, and because of that we were never proactive enough in stopping them.

Slavery and the Thirteenth Amendment

I also believe—as Ruth Bader Ginsburg did—that the right to abortion should not have been argued under the right to privacy, as it was with *Roe v. Wade.* At a 2008 Veteran Feminists of America event honoring Justice Ginsburg, I asked her whether or not lawyers should be working toward recasting the argument of reproductive freedom, changing it from the privacy argument in *Roe* to the Thirteenth Amendment against slavery.

Her response:

> I have criticized the Court's decision in *Roe v. Wade*—not, of course, for the result. But that decision is heavily oriented to doctors. It's the doctor's choice as much as the woman's. The government shouldn't regulate what doctors decide is best for the patient. I think . . . it isn't just some private act; it is a woman's right to control her own life . . . the notion of a woman's autonomy to determine her life's course.

Freud said anatomy is destiny. Elizabeth Hardwick said biology is destiny—but only for girls. I say *Dobbs* has made *geography* destiny.

When a woman is forced, coerced, legislated into carrying a child she does not want, birthing it, and then being responsible for its life for the rest of hers, that is a definition of slavery—the picture of a bond servant. The laws of the state have become the chains of her biology. The idea that there are "safe spaces" is an illusion. There is no safety for women and girls, not even in their own skins. Which is why I say *the power of the state must stop at our skins*.

Laurence Tribe, a leading constitutional scholar, also agreed. As a recent opinion piece by Mike Wilson in the *Lexington Herald Leader* points out: "There is a constitutional basis for a woman's right to terminate a pregnancy the Supreme Court (SCOTUS) has not directly addressed—the 13th Amendment, which abolished slavery and involuntary servitude." Wilson notes that a 1995 Tenth Circuit case, *Jane L. v. Bangerter*, quoted Tribe to support the idea: "A woman forced by law to submit to the pain and anxiety of carrying, delivering, and nurturing a child she does not wish to have is entitled to believe that more than a play on words links her forced labor with the concept of involuntary servitude."[9]

English Philosopher John Locke wrote that all individuals are equal in the sense that they are born with certain "inalienable" natural rights. That is, rights that are God-given and can never be taken or even given away. Among these fundamental natural rights, Locke said, are "life, liberty, and property."

Whose property are women's bodies, if "inalienable" rights are God-given and can never be taken away? Who made women's bodies? The right to decide whether to carry a child to term is an embedded right, a *property* right. Furthermore, it is a sex-based (biological sex) right. It is crucial to make the distinction between that right and other so-called fundamental inalienable rights like the right to assemble and the right to worship, and to realize that it is diminished and politically manipulated just because of this quality.

---

9 Mike Wilson, "Anti-Abortion Laws Constitute Involuntary Servitude That Violates 13th Amendment," *Lexington Herald Leader*, June 1, 2023, https://www.kentucky .com/opinion/op-ed/article275787356.html.

Is a fetus a woman's property? Anita Bernstein in *The Common Law Inside the Female Body* posits a competing narrative to the arguments in *Roe v. Wade.* She argues, "the common law, a source of law usually associated with the interests of conservative, propertied, old white men, is actually a powerful source of liberty for women." In particular, "the common law's central command—that people are free to say 'do not want' with respect to their bodies, property and money—applies to women." Bernstein's application of this central command in two different legal contexts arising "inside the female body" means "the common law protects a right for women to say no to penetration and no to unwanted pregnancy."

Several organizations, such as the World Health Organization (WHO) and Human Rights Watch, prioritize women's reproductive rights over fetal rights. Under European law, a fetus is generally regarded as an *in utero* part of the mother and thus its rights are held by the mother. Rights such as the right to vote, the right to worship, and the right to assemble do not require another person. They don't require a provider or a health care system.

So, this begs the question: Is abortion health care?

Women's bodies bring them into an ongoing and unique relationship with doctors and with the state. Girls are usually brought to see their mother's gynecologist (usually with their mothers) when they start to menstruate, when they need to decide on a birth control device, when they are pregnant and need to make arrangements for a hospital birth, postnatal care, perimenopausal care, menopausal care, post-menopausal care—in fact, women are in continual engagement with gynecologists and the health care system far more frequently than men are.

No one should be forced to carry a pregnancy to term against their will. The ruling from the United States Supreme Court overturning *Roe v. Wade* stripped millions of people of the right to control their bodies and to make the decisions that shape their lives, families, and futures. So yes, one other definition of legal abortion is that it is an integral part of women's health care.

The Supreme Court has now made this inalienable right one that is left to the whims of state legislatures. Now a woman's biology, her destiny, her very relationship to the state is inherently open to manipulation by the state for control—and for power.

When I went to St. Patrick's Cathedral with my proclamation of "Women's Rights are in a State of Emergency," one of the fundamental principles I spoke of was that women are full moral agents with the ability to choose when and whether they want to become mothers. Abortion is a choice made by the individual for profound moral reasons that no man, state, or court can judge. What the *Dobbs* decision does is slam the doors to that personal decision in every woman's face.

The *Dobbs* Decision in Plain Terms

On June 24, 2022, the Supreme Court decided that the Constitution does not confer a right to abortion. Abortion, the argument went, is not mentioned in the Constitution at all, so it is irrelevant on the federal level and must be left up to the states.

I believe that *Roe* was a wise decision about the right to choose. In the first trimester—up to twelve weeks—it was a decision between a woman and her doctor. In the second trimester, the state had a right to regulate, meaning that abortions might have to be done by licensed clinics or by certain credentialed providers depending on individual state health codes. In the third trimester, a woman had the right to an abortion only in order to save the life of the mother or if there were very serious complications with the fetus. In this way, *Roe* expressed the concept that that as the fetus grows, it has a right to demand more legal consideration of the collective society.

Not being satisfied with this legal compromise, *Dobbs* opens the door to pass laws that give equal rights to fetuses which, in some cases, trump a woman's right to life altogether. But there are no absolutes anywhere outside of mathematics. A philosophy that leaves no room for debate, or for nuance, smacks of a religious conviction more than anything. Some doctors, like Dr. Warren Hern, embrace an absolutism of a different sort. Dr. Hern has been performing late-term abortions for half a century and continues to do so after *Dobbs* at his clinic in Colorado. In his eighty-three years of life, he has been the target of violence, his family has been stalked and threatened, his clinic vandalized, and his friends murdered—but he continues to perform abortions.

"Every totalitarian regime has shut down access to reproductive health," he said. "Doing abortions matters for the woman, for her family, for society, and now for freedom."[10] Recalling telling an early patient she was no longer pregnant, Hern was "overwhelmed by the significance of the operation for this young woman's life." I have experienced this many times—the profound power of giving someone their life back. In Hern's view, an abortion is a "surgical procedure for a life-threatening condition."

"Every pregnancy is a health issue!" he recently told *The Atlantic*.[11] "There's a certifiable risk of death from being pregnant, period." The title of the piece in *The Atlantic* refers to Hern as "the abortion absolutist" and in a way, Hern's position—political, polemic, and psychological—is translated into a personal theoretical manifesto that gets operationalized through his role as a physician. And how can one be an "absolutist" in anything, particularly abortion?

The *Dobbs* decision throws out the wisdom of *Roe* and says there is no law or federal understanding of when and how and where women can access the right to safe, legal abortion. It is, instead, totally dependent on where she is living because it is up to the states to adjudicate. With *Dobbs*, geography really is destiny. If you live in Texas and the state legislature bans all abortions after six weeks, that is your bad luck. Such is the wisdom of *Dobbs*. When I was young, before legal abortion, when my dreams of being a great concert pianist ruled my waking hours, the idea that my body would betray me and that I'd have to give up all my

---

10 Molly Hennessy-Fiske, "As a med student, he saw women nearly die from illegal abortions. At 83, he sees no end to his work," *Los Angeles Times*, March 10, 2022, https://www.latimes.com/world-nation/story/2022–03-10/abortion-doctor-fears-roes-fall.
11 Elaine Godfrey, "The Abortion Absolutist," *Atlantic*, May 12, 2023, https://www.theatlantic.com/politics/archive/2023/05/dr-warren-hern-abortion-post-roe/674000/.

dreams for my future because of some sexual interlude was terrifying. I remember *praying* for my period to come. Not having the right and the access to safe, legal abortion kills one's autonomy and one's dreams.

According to Greek myth, Pandora had a box filled with evils. When she curiously opened the box, all the evils flew into the world. She slammed the box shut and one evil remained—hope. And in some sense, it is hope that got us here. Depending on your worldview, hope can be a positive or negative thing. In the case of the mainstream pro-choice movement, their expectation that "they would never take away *Roe*"—that perhaps Justice Roberts would be able to keep abortion legal up to fifteen weeks—led to a tepid response that focused on compromise and ultimately surrender.

Jean-Jacques Rousseau, who had produced the bible of the French Revolution, *The Social Contract* (which began: "Man is born free and everywhere he is in chains"), believed everything was socially constructed. (Rousseau, who theorized that much of what we call "reality" and "human nature" is created by the language we use to describe it, could be viewed as the father of the entire de-constructionist movement. This is the theoretical foundation underlying the thinking of some of the feminist movement and much of the "woke" movement.)

But pregnancy, childbirth, and abortion are not socially constructed. Thinking that they are leads us to cede to the opposition the narrative of what abortion is, does, and means. The problem with the mainstream pro-choice movement is that they really did not believe what the right-wing anti-abortion movement kept saying. The Antis believed it wholeheartedly. We wanted and continue to want to be able to debate, to reason, to compromise. But we are fighting God's chosen warriors, and that approach is a terrible tactical and strategic weakness. We can talk and talk; meanwhile, the opposition never stopped believing and never stopped moving.

While we were downplaying the threat, the Antis were busy establishing so-called trigger laws in several states. The trigger laws were set up in such a way that should *Roe* be overturned—and they knew it was only a matter of time until it was—and the federal protection for abortion rights fell, the states would have anti-abortion laws that went into effect immediately. Within months of the *Dobbs* decision, two or three states had total abortion bans in place. Those laws were appealed, of course, but the result is the same: a patchwork quilt of continual appeals and struggles on the state level. That is how the anti-abortion agenda gets normalized, and that alone is a major victory for the Antis.

After *Dobbs*: The Decision and the Real-World Ramifications

This cruel indifference to women and children isn't a byproduct of these bans and the overturning of *Roe*—it is the reason for them. For instance, it would reasonable to assume that "pro-life" and pro-choice forces should agree on the need for better sex education and birth control because it would reduce the number of unplanned and unwanted pregnancies. But from the first debate I did with Dr. Mildred Jefferson, the first Black woman to graduate from Harvard medical school, over forty years ago, the response was always that most birth control kills babies—the "pill is chemical warfare." You can hear echoes of this today in criminal prosecutions for murder of women who are drug users.[12] As of 2018, thirty-eight states had laws in which the "victim" of a crime includes the fetus. These laws are usually termed fetal protection laws, but they are really used to punish individuals for a wide range of behaviors that include attempting suicide, substance abuse, and a suspicion of self-managed abortions. ACOG (American College of Obstetricians and Gynecologists) has opposed these types of laws, but unfortunately they continue to remain in place. ACOG has stated that a pregnant person has the right to refuse medical treatment. In other words, patients can't be forced into accepting

---

12 Emma Coleman, "Many States Prosecute Pregnant Women for Drug Use. New Research Says That's a Bad Idea," Vanderbilt University Medical Center, December 5, 2019, https://www.vumc.org/childhealthpolicy/news-events/many-states-prosecute -pregnant-women-dr"ug-use-new-research-says-thats-bad-idea.

a treatment because evidence-based medicine shows us that this treatment is the best for themselves and/or the fetus.

The real threat legal abortion poses is the realization that women—like men—can have a chosen sexual life without risking their entire futures. (Although in many cases they still risk their "reputations.") Women could actualize their dreams and perhaps become anything they wanted if they had the ambition and the skills. They also began to take jobs that were generally held by men, creating what many analysts consider an underlying reason for the current rise in expressed misogyny in our society.

In the last fifty years, the number of women who have gone into law, medicine, banking, and corporate leadership has grown enormously. The fact that this revolution in women's participation in society was so tied to their ability to decide when and whether to be mothers was the most critical part of this change. Women's autonomy is the most threatening to the power structure, which is still predominantly male. This is why women and their reproduction had to be controlled. This is why the Antis fought so hard to overturn *Roe* and replace it with a religious, repressive, and *regressive* vision.

Dobbs asks the health care system to stretch and accommodate new laws, which, like the system in Kafka's "In the Penal Colony," are more concerned with upholding power than they are with the dignity of human life. In Kafka's story, it takes twelve hours to finish an execution by repeatedly etching the prisoner's sentence into his flesh. So similar are the various torture machines of *Dobbs*, which utilize the medical "judgments" of doctors to decide questions of how close a woman must be to death to allow her a "life-saving" abortion.

We have entered a Kafkaesque reality where women's bodies and lives inhabit a deep dystopian existence. The immediate and real-world ramifications of *Dobbs* are shockingly cruel. There was a case of a woman walking around with a headless fetus because she couldn't get an abortion. Or the ten-year-old Ohio child who was raped by a family member and had to go to Indiana, because she was three days over six weeks pregnant.

Immediately after *Dobbs*, the staff at Choices was quite emotional and upset. Some were crying, others were mumbling different iterations of "those fucking bastards." I had meetings with many of them in groups and spoke with some individually. I told them we've been here since the beginning, we're historic, we're the standard, we are going to stand. We are going to help every woman that comes here, and we are going to be strong. I gave one of my battle speeches. And I delivered the same message I delivered so many times in those days. In the words of Joe Hill, the labor organizer: "Don't waste any time mourning. Organize!"

They rose to the occasion and continue to do so every day. Many of the patients we began to see from out of state had never been on a plane before. These were young women, many coming for later-term abortions who, fortunately, had received the funds from volunteer feminist and newly assembled nonprofit organizations to travel to New York. But the fear is profound, almost tangible. Not only do they feel as though they are doing something illegal, but they believe themselves to be immoral as well. The Antis have been very effective in this way. They have created a narrative in which anyone who gets an abortion is bad—a sinner, an evil person. One cruelty upon another.

I understand that it is easier *not* to confront, *not* to have uncomfortable conversations again and again, but that is the nature of this struggle. You have to be confrontational. You have to call out what is happening as it is happening. When nobody is standing up or screaming "STOP," the opposition will simply keep going, which is exactly what they did.

What Happened in Kansas?

Soon after *Dobbs*, attention turned to upcoming elections. Confidence that the Supreme Court was a reflection of public opinion was put to the test almost right away in the state of Kansas, where a referendum was to be held on August 2, 2022. The Value Them Both constitutional amendment had been approved for a vote a year before *Dobbs* came down. If passed, the amendment would remove Kansas's constitutional protections for abortion, allowing the state to enact more restrictions.

Of course, we knew that public opinion was *not* with the *Dobbs* decision, and that the Supreme Court was illegitimate, so we were watching carefully. Crucially, the referendum in Kansas was the first time post-*Dobbs* that the question would be put directly to the people. Voter registration in Kansas surged after *Dobbs*, particularly among Democratic and female voters. Significantly, Kansas voters ultimately rejected the proposed constitutional amendment, with almost 60 percent of voters voting "No."

These results also reflected the strong strain of individualism in this country. Over the years, many people have said to me, "I don't like abortion. In fact, I'm against it, but I'll be damned if I'm going to let the government tell me what to do." Additionally, people are often not open about their pro-choice beliefs—not with their families or with friends. But when they go into the voting booth, the truth comes out. Every major poll continues to show the majority of Americans hold pro-choice beliefs. There are significant differences of opinion within the question, and it's a profound and complex issue, but the fact remains: most Americans support the right to choose.

Many people on both sides were positively surprised by the vote in Kansas, but there was no real sigh of relief. (Would there be a sigh of relief if a referendum on the right to free speech didn't pass? No.) A fundamental right must transcend a state's rights approach; it cannot be something up for a vote every other election. We should consider a continuous, never-ending state-by-state fight—even with some wins—a loss. The problem is that as we fight those ever-changing battles, we must always keep our eye on the prize: legal abortion nationwide.

Midterms: Be Careful What You Wish For

Following in Kansas's footsteps, voters in that year's midterm elections came out overwhelmingly in support of abortion rights. There were multiple analyses done on the post-*Dobbs* midterm elections. What they have shown is that a combination of more women, more *Democratic* women, and young voters came out to secure the reproductive rights under threat. This crossed party lines, too. In Kansas, many voters voted both for reproductive rights *and* Republican candidates.

The midterm elections illustrated how significant *Dobbs* was, with voters helping Democrats retain control of the Senate. In every state in which abortion was on the ballot, voters voted against bans or restrictions. *Dobbs,* reported the *Guardian,* "drove a surge in voter registration, especially for Democrats, and it made abortion rights a more salient voting issue." That "translated into results."[13] A 2022 PEW Research Center poll on abortion found that "[o]verall, just 7 percent of all US adults say abortion is morally acceptable in all cases, and 13 percent say it is morally wrong in all cases. A third say that abortion is morally wrong in *most* cases, while about a quarter (24 percent) say it is morally acceptable most of the time. About an additional one-in-five do not consider abortion a moral issue." The poll also found that "among religiously unaffiliated Americans, about three-quarters see abortion as morally acceptable (45 percent) or not a moral issue (32 percent)."[14]

As the *Nation* pointed out, overturning *Roe* was the "culmination" of a nearly forty-year GOP project. But the issue won't simply go away. "Republican strategists naturally want voters to move on from the abortion issue. That's because, despite their bluster before the midterms, they know voters care about the issue—and support reproductive freedom by a strong majority."[15]

As recent as the spring of 2023, pushback against abortion bans was felt in elections in South Carolina, Nebraska,

---

13 Melody Schreiber, "'We're Doubling Down': How Abortion Advocates Are Building On Midterm Wins," *Guardian*, December 7, 2022, https://www.theguardian .com/world/2022/dec/07/abortion-supporters-building-midterm-wins.

14 Pew Research Center, "America's Abortion Quandary, 2. Social and moral considerations on abortion," May 6, 2022, https://www.pewresearch.org/religion /2022/05/06/social-and-moral-considerations-on-abortion/.

15 Jeet Heer, "Be Careful What You Work For: The GOP's Abortion Woes Are Just Starting," *Nation*, November 21, 2022, https://www.thenation.com/article/politics /gop-abortion-realignment-midterms/.

and Wisconsin. In August 2023, voters in Ohio overwhelmingly rejected a GOP-engineered referendum to raise the threshold needed to pass constitutional amendments from a simple majority to 60 percent. The true purpose of this measure was not, as Republicans claimed, to safeguard the state constitution, but to block an upcoming vote on an abortion-rights amendment scheduled to be on the ballot in November. It was not only a significant victory for abortion-rights advocates but yet another in a wave of state-level setbacks for the anti-abortion movement. The Antis are now in the process of figuring out how to reposition themselves. *Dobbs* threw the decision back to the states, and it is at the state level where we must fight and defeat them. But what they really want is a national ban.

The International Ripple

The response to *Dobbs* can be seen abroad, too. The anti-abortion push in the US has metastasized internationally, where right-wing governments are pushing back against women's rights. Andrea Peto, writing in *Le Monde*, says, "from Hungary to Poland, from Germany to Denmark and Russia to Serbia, mothers and their beautiful fair-skinned babies smile at us from expensive advertising posters praising motherhood and explicitly condemning abortion."

The New York Times reported how lawmakers in France "backed a proposal to enshrine abortion rights in the country's Constitution, in a move devised as a direct response to the US Supreme Court's decision to overturn *Roe v. Wade*."[16] But as there has been movement toward liberalization in some places around the world, this has also brought pushback from the anti-abortion forces. In Poland in November 2020, thousands poured into the streets, disrupting business as usual and denouncing the

---

16 Constant Méheut, "French Lawmakers Back Bill to Enshrine Abortion Rights in Constitution," *New York Times*, November 24, 2022, https://www.nytimes.com/2022/11/24/world/europe/france-abortion-rights-constitution.html.

government's new ban on abortion. They carried symbols of red thunderbolts, umbrellas, and wire coat hangers—hangers!—that universal symbol of dangerous, illegal abortions they refused to accept (unlike Planned Parenthood, who I had to fight for them to consider using the hanger a symbol, and other groups within the pro-choice coalition who were afraid to confront the reality). I wrote a letter of support, which was printed in the largest newspaper in Poland.

I wrote:

To the Great Women of Poland,

The world is in awe of your principled activism and is filled with admiration for your courage and commitment. American Feminists stand with you. We salute and support you with love and pride. You have marched by the thousands in response to the October 22nd Tribunal ruling which denied abortion even in cases of fetal abnormality in what has been called the largest demonstration in the country since the fall of communism.

Ignoring threats of prosecution, violence from the Right, and the dangers posed by a surging Coronavirus, while displaying symbols of Red Thunderbolts, Hangers, and Umbrellas, your resistance intensifies daily. You have challenged formerly "untouchable" institutions and are a stellar example of what people everywhere need to do in the fight against oppression and for women's freedom.

We stand with you in solidarity.

The letter was signed by a plethora of known feminists, including Phyllis Chesler, Gloria Steinem, and Naomi Wolf.

Unfortunately, things have only gotten worse in Poland. According to *Al Jazeera*: "Thousands of people have demonstrated across Poland against the country's restrictive abortion law after a woman who was five months pregnant died of sepsis, the latest such death since a tightening of the law. Protesters chanted 'Stop killing us' as they marched through the capital Warsaw towards the health ministry headquarters, some carrying placards that said, WE WANT DOCTORS, NOT MISSIONARIES and HELL FOR WOMEN, a common slogan used to convey how the measure affects those who are carrying an unwanted or dangerous pregnancy."[17]

When I see the passion and crowds in Poland using slogans that tell it like it is—"STOP KILLING US"—this should serve as an inspiration for American feminists and people of conscience to get out in the streets! Everyone must recognize the critical role of activists and advocates around the world who consistently oppose and resist the realities of state theocratic control of women's bodies and lives. While it is possible to look at global trends and find positive movement, the *Dobbs* decision will have a disproportionate negative impact because of the past role of the United States as a leader on Women's Health and Reproductive Justice.

One article, published in the journal *Sexual and Reproductive Health Matters,* about the global impact of *Dobbs* and abortion rights degeneration in the US, concluded that "the regressive and harmful decision in *Dobbs v. Jackson Women's Health Organization* stands in stark contrast to the overwhelming trend toward global progress on abortion rights and access. As we anticipate the emboldening impact that the ruling may have on opposition forces around the world, it is critical that advocates emphasize the movement successes and legal and policy advances in abortion rights over the past twenty-five years. These advances and the movements that made them possible should serve to isolate the decision as out of step with human rights and the global trend of liberalization."

As devastating as the impacts of the decision will be, access to safe abortion care is a critical issue far beyond the US's borders. Globally, particularly in fragile and conflict-affected countries, unsafe abortions are a leading cause of maternal death. These deaths are far more common where abortion is heavily restricted or banned. We may be out of step with the global trend

---

17 "Thousands protest against strict abortion law in Poland," *Al Jazeera*, June 14, 2023, https://www.aljazeera.com/news/2023/6/14/thousands-protest-strict-abortion -law-after-pregnant-woman-dies.

of liberalization, but we are marching right on with the right-wing governments around the world.

We had the opening to align ourselves with other progressive nations decades ago, but failed to do so when we allowed the Hyde Amendment to pass in 1976, effectively cutting Medicaid funds for poor women's abortions. We continue to uphold Hyde to this day, despite many opportunities to strike it down. In fact, Hyde comes up in the Budget Reconciliation Act every year. As I write now all these years later, the Hyde Amendment still stands. No matter who is in the White House—Republican, Democrat, Trump, Biden (who now declares himself a warrior for choice because, as he stated in his speech on the first anniversary of *Dobbs*, it "really matters")—the Hyde Amendment is kept in. Why? Because we are held hostage to politics. Obama, for example, had to get the votes of a few Catholics for his Affordable Care Act. He had to capitulate; everyone does. Poor and minority women don't have a voice, so they become the low-hanging fruit—the casualties of "working across the aisle."

Within months, we had our first Hyde Amendment death— Rosie Jimenez, a young Mexican American woman killed by a botched illegal abortion in Mexico because her Medicaid coverage was cut off in Texas. A few years later, I spoke at a house meeting in Queens to a group of young married women who had given up careers to stay home with their first babies. They were uncomfortable with me—uptight, curious, impressed, and threatened—newly rationalized in their roles. I spoke of the cutoff of Medicaid funds for abortions that would so badly affect poor women. It was not their problem. If abortion rights were cut off for everybody, they could after all fly to those abortion havens in Puerto Rico, England, Sweden . . . anywhere. They had the money. No coat hangers, bottles, and back alleys for them. They were not poor, and they were White.

Cutting through a deafening pro-choice silence, a small but fervent right-to-life movement began to coalesce around the issue.[18] They began to harass and terrorize patients and providers,

18 Founded eight years earlier in 1968, the National Right to Life Committee is the oldest and largest national anti-abortion organization, with affiliates in all fifty states.

and began chipping away at the supply side of the abortion equation. Starting with street harassment, which they labeled "sidewalk counseling," to eventually entering the clinics themselves.

One of the most aggressive and challenging actions happened at a Planned Parenthood Center in Manhattan, when Operation Rescue activists (including priests) chained themselves in concrete collars to chairs. There, they sat in a room full of women waiting to have their abortions, saying things like "There'll be no killing here today, you all best go home" and "No babies will die here today." It took the police about two hours to saw through those collars, and the session for that day had to be canceled. I know how long it took because I was inside waiting for the police to come. The pro-choice forces failed to stop the Antis from invading the clinic, so I and a few others stayed with the patients in the waiting room—to attempt to buffer the psychological assault they were under.

With Operation Rescue, the most common tactic is to form a human blockade outside an abortion clinic. Protesters sometimes chain themselves together with bicycle locks or to their cars to make it harder for police to remove them. Sometimes, the protesters pour glue into door locks, write anti-abortion slogans on clinic property, or strew nails on a clinic's parking lot. On occasion, they have entered clinics and destroyed equipment used for abortions.

Unlike the terrorist tactics of Operation Rescue, the political argument around abortion is centered around "choice." The reproductive justice movement asks the question: How can one realistically choose when for so many, especially the Black and minority populations, the choice is a forgone conclusion and made out of economic necessity and for survival? Interestingly enough, with *Roe v. Wade* in the background giving women the opportunity not to be pregnant, for many women, the act of continuing a pregnancy is more of a "choice" than it ever was historically. But "choice" is a contextual word. For some who have money and means, it is an available possibility. But for others, like my patients who depended on Medicaid, how can one speak of choice when there is no financial support, no economic security, no comprehensive prenatal or general health care? For the poorest women, "choice" is a total misnomer.

Some believe that context is irrelevant, and that the choice of abortion is wrong for whatever reason in all places at any time. But attitudes about abortion are situational, historic, and geographical. My work in the early 1990s to open Choices East, a satellite of Choices Women's Medical Center, in the former Soviet Union was inspired by a thirty-five-year-old woman who came to our medical center for her thirty-sixth abortion.

Like so many other Russian émigré women living in New York, she was violently opposed to using birth control because her Russian doctor taught her that "the pill" was far more dangerous than repeat abortions. This misinformation benefited Russian physicians because they could earn extra money doing abortions on women in their homes to supplement their three-dollars-a-month salary. Other forms of contraception were unavailable for all practical purposes. (Condoms were available, but they were so thick the Russians called them "galoshes.") For these women, the "issue" of abortion posed no questions of morality, ethics, or women's rights versus fetal life. There was only the harsh reality that sex rarely came without anxiety and that the price one often paid for it was high and dangerous.

Are these women who have no other choice continually making the wrong one? Are the women of Egypt, Iraq, El Salvador, and others, who are so much a product of their paternalistic and misogynistic cultures, making the wrong choice when they want a child who will not join their husband's families after marriage, or when they want sons to take care of parents as they age, as are the practices in their societies? Are they making the wrong choice if the results of their choice determine their ability and their family's ability to survive? When and where is a choice right or wrong? And according to who?

The Chooser and the Choice

Yes, life. Who decides? Who benefits and who loses? And at what cost?

My mind goes to a TV debate I participated in. *Here it comes again*, I thought. The slippery slope argument—that abortion is the gateway sin to all others. That time it came from a woman, a nurse, a leader of the Anti movement in New York: Jean Head.

"Once you allow abortion," she said, "once you say a life is worthless in the womb, what is to stop you from killing once it is born? It is a short step from abortion to live baby killing."

These decisions are often so wrenching and profound that they must rest with the mother as opposed to a hospital committee or an anti-choice guardian ad litem. Consider the case of a severely deformed baby girl lying in a hospital with very little chance for a life of anything but pain.

The parents of little "Baby Jane Doe" did not make their choice easily. Baby Doe was a wanted child for the young, Catholic, Long Island couple. Born severely handicapped, the only correctable deformity was her spina bifida. With surgery she might live to twenty. Because of her deformities, she would be unaware of life around her, with, according to the physician in charge of the case, "only a limited ability to experience comfort, and primarily an ability to experience pain."

"To perform this surgery," he said, "would increase the total pain that the child would experience." After consulting with a number of physicians, their families, and clergy, the couple, in great pain themselves, decided to oppose surgery for their daughter. Then the Antis stepped in and appointed a guardian for the child. When they were defeated by the courts, they refused to let go. On their heels came the Reagan administration; special interest groups began to take sides. The Antis found this an ideal case for their "slippery slope" argument that the legalization of abortion leads directly to euthanasia and the murder of live infants.

The profound nature of the moral choice that these parents must make should not be controlled by government intervention. It may be true that the ultimate act of love for these loving parents, their ultimate expression of parental protection, can only be shown in letting their daughter die rather than suffer needlessly. It is, certainly, a decision that they alone—not the press, not the state, not the hospital, not the physicians—have to live with and think about alone in bed at night.

Recall the Florida woman forced to carry an unviable fetus to term after the state's fifteen-week abortion ban went into effect. While the law has an exception for fetal abnormalities, because the baby's heart continued to beat, the mother had no choice but to deliver. Baby Milo was expected to live for less than two hours. He died ninety-nine minutes after he was born.

Women. Choice. Victims. Little girls. Parents. Fetuses. Abortion. Life. Words to most people. But for me, these are everyday realities. There are no easy answers here. Only the intensity and demands of this commitment and the knowledge of how important it all is. The unasked, unanswered, and unanswerable questions. My work, the work all of us must do—to begin the momentous task of rebuilding.

A New Enemy

Abortion did not become the partisan issue we see today until Republicans began to reach out to Catholic voters with a pro-family platform. This was after the fall of the Berlin Wall in 1989, when another major enemy was needed to focus energy and funds for American conservatives and the Republican Party. Only then did abortion truly become a rallying cry for the right—the banner they would march under. "The empire we are fighting"—the abortion industry—"is every bit as evil as Empire of the Soviet Union," said Patrick Buchanan, a Republican candidate for president in 1992.

Since that watershed moment, and throughout the following decades, abortion has become a defining political problem, surfacing as both a wedge issue and a major fundraising possibility. Of course, feminists and the pro-choice movement have always called for policies that support women, children, and mothers, yet the US has the highest rates of preventable maternal mortality among similarly developed countries, while pregnancy outcomes for Black and minority women are even worse than in some third world countries. As far as general health care is concerned, the US trails far behind other high-income countries on measures of affordability, administrative efficiency, equity, and outcome. So much for the Right's claim to be "pro-life" or any definition of "pro-natal."

My theme from the Hyde Amendment of a Women's Rights State of Emergency was one I reprised in 1989 in front of St. Patrick's Cathedral at the first Pro-Choice Civil Disobedience Action, during which nine people were arrested. This was in direct response to the attacks and invasions by Operation Rescue in New York which then-Cardinal O'Connor had given his blessing to. The slogan of the group was: "If you believe abortion is murder, act like it's murder." I had *armed* guards sent by Janet Reno to protect me at the clinic because of the death threats. Once again, I was calling on people to stand up and *do* something.

Beyond terrorist attacks, harassment, and death threats, the anti-abortion movement would pursue quieter strategies over the decades that followed. By the time the *Dobbs* decision came down, a number of states had slowly but carefully regressed and passed laws restricting abortions. We were already seeing patients from out of state before *Dobbs*, either because they couldn't get a later-term abortion, there were other problems with referrals, or for any number of other reasons. It had been happening for quite some time, right in front of our faces. I've said many times: one should never minimize the opposition. You have to respect your opponent—not their ideology, but the fact they, too, are fighting for what they believe in. Since they are fighting for what they believe in, they are persistent and relentless.

But again, this requires a degree of empathic imagination—a lessening of "otherness." Rather than trying to understand them through a progressive lens or as an enormous "basket of deplorables," which could lead to capitulation or some ill-advised compromise, we must understand them to strategize proactive tactics in this ongoing war. This understanding requires a degree of respect for the "otherness" of the Antis' worldview because it is so antithetical to ours, and is always diminished to our detriment. The dependence on *Roe* and the shock expressed by so many when *Dobbs* came should serve as a profound lesson on progressive collective denial. We made fun of the little plastic fetuses that the Antis wore as lapel pins, of their metaphorical burial grounds with tiny crosses. But they were deadly earnest. Recently in Arkansas, there has been a call to build a Monument to the Unborn. We should take it seriously.

The passage of *Roe v. Wade* was considered a great victory for women in general and for the feminist movement in particular. In the beginning, working in or being part of an abortion clinic was the closest that any feminist could come to living in Utopia. Of course, outside of marching and going to meetings to plan actions, there was a reality on the ground: real women accessing legal safe abortion. What had been a sin—a criminal act—now became a kind of rite of passage. Thousands of women were lining up to have an abortion as soon as it was legalized in New York. Again, this made me ask myself the question: how many women who were pregnant for all those decades and centuries when there was no access to legal safe abortion really "wanted" those children that they birthed?

If you accept the reality that abortion is the termination of *potential* life (an acorn is not a tree), abortion is both a power *and* a survival decision. As the saying goes, "Feminism is the theory; abortion is the practice." The authority over life and death when it comes to war or criminal justice is made by the existing power structure. Men made the decisions about life and death and war; women made the decision about abortion. That is why it is such a profound power struggle.

What was lost in the years after *Roe* was the authentic link between the providers who, often at the risk of their lives, serve the women who come for abortions, and the national organizations who shape national political pro-choice strategy. "Doing" abortions instead of fighting for the right to have them slowly bifurcated into separate worlds. I recall a cocktail party at Peggy Guggenheim's Sutton Place apartment where we had an engaged conversation about the current struggle over "second trimester" abortions. At one point I referred to the practice at Choices. She looked at me with a combination of surprise and disgust and said, "You don't *do those*—do you?"

The feminist movement had an enormous challenge—to rethink, reclarify, and redefine our relationships with non-feminist-identified women. To consider traditional feminist politics only in the genre of electoral politics is a grave error.

There is a reason why the anti-choice movement counted and still counts so many women in its ranks. Phyllis Schlafly, who is credited with having a major role in preventing the passage of the Equal Rights Amendment, should not have been dismissed as an antediluvian aberration. She was also primarily concerned with power. Her perceptions of how women should achieve and use their power lay in the historically based role of woman as reproducer of children, as homemaker, as mentor to the next generation of active and responsible citizens. For many women this was a profound reinforcement of their belief systems as well as their lived lives. Schlafly's organization at its height had far more members than the National Organization of Women. Schlafly herself was a fireball of ambition and energy with many accomplishments.

Until this distinction between women of the anti-choice movement and the pro-choice movement is recognized for what it really is—that is, different definitions of female power and the boundaries of its use—women will continue to be politically divided based on a fabricated reality and ultimately serve only the interests of a repressive establishment.

Abortion is a *mother's act*. Statistically, the majority of women who have abortions already have at least one child. Across race, culture, geography, and class, this ability to reproduce, and the power and vulnerability that comes with it, is the glue that binds all women. I have often said and written that if women cannot control (have power over) their own reproductive lives (themselves), that they can never hope to control, direct, or have power over anything else. At the core of the feminist line is a call to power and, therefore, to greater responsibility. "Power" for most women is a dirty word, unacceptable to "good girls" who have not been trained or conditioned in its acceptance or usage.

I had seen so much of this every day at Choices. Numerous women of all ages who so eagerly put their biological life choices into the hands of men.

"He wants me to stop using the pill."

"He said it was my safe period."

"He says using a rubber is like wearing a glove."

"He said he could feel my diaphragm, so I didn't use it."

"He wants a boy."

Here, too, is an example of the "enemy having outposts in our heads." These outposts include the stigma that abortion still carries. Never mind all the T-shirts saying I HAD AN ABORTION, there are still millions of women who have had legal, safe abortions—sometimes more than one—and are too filled with shame to talk about them.

Over the years, as legal abortion became normalized, the feminist movement made major inroads on other pressing issues—rape, domestic violence, racism in the movement, worker's rights, pay equity, etc. At the same time, clinics were facing more dangerous and sometimes fatal attacks. There was not so much theorizing or writing about abortion either—after all, it was "settled law." Now that it was legal, they wanted to turn their eyes to other issues. This thinking only intensified as clinics were further cast out in the eyes of the medical establishment. We were seen as outside the system—beneath it. When the clinics started to be attacked by opposition terrorists, the majority of the feminist movement distanced itself even further.

As a provider and activist publisher, I was one of the few people who were deeply involved in both worlds. I knew all the players in all parts of the movement. I was always involved in the discussions. Yet, after *Roe*, the feminist movement wasn't talking or writing about abortion as much. Within a few short years, we—the independent clinics, their providers, and their staff—were very much on our own.

CHAPTER 4
THE RISE OF THE ANTIS

Two Camps

On the surface, one could say there are two "camps" in the struggle over abortion—pro-choice and anti-choice (aka Antis). These two groups live in two very distinct and different worlds, and bridging the gap between them is a great challenge. We are not dealing with a clash of facts, or a debate about reality, but a clash of civilizations, cultures, and differing views of reality. It is a mistake to think of the anti-choice movement as a singular entity motivated and driven by a singular philosophy. As in the pro-choice movement, there are moderates, radicals, religious people, and academics. There are those who would settle for a six-week abortion ban and those who would demand the death penalty for women who choose abortion.

These distinctions minimize the glue that holds all of these factions together—primarily the ability to subsume individual ego needs to a higher authority. Many Antis consider themselves to be doing God's work and are comfortable playing a part in what they view as a biblical struggle. This point of view enables them to perceive time in a different manner: epochs as opposed to elections. You can present Antis with all the scientific experiential data in the world, but they will insist it is propaganda. They will insist the issue and information are being politicized. They ultimately strive for a time when the very idea of abortion would be odious, when just thinking about an abortion would be a sin akin to "lusting in your heart."

When Kate Michelman, former executive director of the National Abortion Rights Action League (NARAL), is quoted saying that "We think abortion is a bad thing"; when almost-Surgeon General Dr. Henry Foster calls it "abhorrent" and a "failure"; and when feminist "icon" Hillary Rodham Clinton describes it as "morally wrong"; they sidestep abortion's messy reality, which is grounded in women's lives, and act as a silencing force that inhibits women from telling the truth. Comments like these serve to reinforce the outposts in our heads, but they are coming from *our side*.

In what he defined as a "principled-yet-pragmatic stand," anti-choice author George McKenna argued that the best way to ultimately eliminate abortion was to adopt a "politics of civility" that is simultaneously anti-abortion and accepting of contemporary abortion law. Addressing anti-choice politicians, he advised taking a position similar to the one Lincoln adopted on slavery well into the Civil War—tolerate, restrict, discourage.

In McKenna's analysis, the pro-choice movement is comparable to the pro-slavery forces who supported an immoral institution by claiming freedom of choice while not facing the reality of what they were choosing. Calling abortion "the corpse at the dinner table," he believed it had come to occupy a surrealistic place in the national dialogue. Using Kate Michelman's comments to support his analysis that abortion in the 1990s—like slavery in the 1850s—was the sin that cannot speak its name, he argued that for the time being pro-lifers should accept the legality but not the moral legitimacy of abortion.

Just as slavery was ultimately abolished, legal abortion (which McKenna defines as evil) has also passed into history through slow-weaning processes of regulation, restrictions, and social pressure. Not surprisingly, women did not figure much in McKenna's worldview except as confused and misinformed patients of abortion providers. The stark reality of enforced pregnancy as a category of slavery was never explored. For McKenna, fetuses=slaves and women=nothing.

What's God Got to Do with It?

I was brought up socially and culturally Jewish but never went to Hebrew school and did not receive a traditional Jewish education. I loved the holidays and celebrations because of the time it allowed me to spend with family. As an only child, sitting at those large tables with all my cousins was like being inside of my own Norman Rockwell painting. But I have always been curious about other forms of worship, too. When I discovered Mary Queen of Scots, I wanted to become a Catholic. I loved the rosaries, the smell of the churches, and the spiritual paraphernalia. I studied with the Christian scientists and went to a "practitioner"—a kind of counselor/therapist who advises you according to the philosophy of Mary Baker Eddy, an American religious leader who founded the Church of Christ, Scientist in 1879. I used to go to group meetings where people would testify as to how they actually cured themselves of very serious disease. These meetings were not in a tent or in some rural area on the outskirts of the city, but on the Upper East Side of Manhattan. Many of the congregants were high-functioning professional individuals.

I attended the Church of Truth at Lincoln Center every Sunday for a year. I remember the message as uplifting and positive. I welcomed Jehovah's Witnesses into my home and sat and listened to them. I once went in person to Madison Square Garden to see one of the famous Evangelical preachers and got a whiff of the real-time energy of that experience.

I would even listen to the Sunday morning preachers on TV. I remember my husband yelling at me to "turn that shit off." But I knew that, in listening, I was learning about the opposition.

I do believe that one can always find wisdom, or even a kernel of truth, in the most unexpected of places. Personally, however, I have never found a home in any of these religious spaces, nor in the writings of the new atheists like Christopher Hitchens and Richard Dawkins. I ponder the possibility of the existence of God regularly and follow the new theories on the connections between the scientific and religious communities. What has historically been thought of as two competing theories of the architecture of reality are now in conversation with each other. As Einstein said, "God does not throw dice."

Pro-choice religious leaders of all faiths are now much more aggressive in stating their beliefs. According to *Politico*, since the fall of *Roe*, there have been multiple challenges filed by members of the reform and conservative arms of Judaism and Islam along with clergy from other religions, including Satanism.

In Indiana, the arguments the plaintiffs use are the ones the Antis have used to buffer their own bans and restrictions—basically that *Dobbs* violates the Religious Freedom Restoration Act signed into law by then-governor Mike Pence in 2015. Conservatives argue that these efforts are doomed to fail and often quote Ruth Bader Ginsburg when ruling in a free exercise of religion case that "the right to swing your arm ends just where the other man's nose begins." Yet, this counterargument assumes that the fetus is a person—a religious/political/philosophical question that leads us back to the same place where the fetus will command more rights than the woman who carries it.

I have concluded that I am comfortable living with these existential questions, and if I knew the answer it would not change my behavior at all. As Martin Buber says, it is how one lives in the world, how one interacts and reacts with others, that is profoundly important.

No Conviction without Action

Curiosity once led me to attend a right-to-life convention with Bill Baird in the early eighties. There, I marched outside with him under a large wooden cross with the words SAVE WOMEN FROM THE CROSS OF RELIGIOUS OPPRESSION.

Inside, one of the keynote speakers, an Australian priest, was speaking to a hushed and diffident audience. He, too, was a martyr . . . fasting for ten days in a public square to "get in touch with the helplessness and defenselessness of the fetus." A slide show: a funeral, a small casket, hundreds of marchers carrying one rose, tears, speeches, an interment. Mary Elizabeth—posthumously named and celebrated—a four-month fetus rescued from a garbage can, a victim of the "abortion holocaust." Stirring words appeared on top of a little pad of notepaper in a conference kit:

"THERE IS NO CONVICTION WITHOUT ACTION."—CARLYLE.

I moved through the crowd slowly, stopping at booths. It was just like any other conference, only not. It was another reality, another world. I was a stranger in a strange land. Fetuses in bottles of formaldehyde. Mother of pearl pins on lapels. I looked closer. It was their logo . . . tiny feet . . . fetal feet . . . mother of pearl fetal feet. $3.00.

Feminists for Life engaged me in debate. "You," they charged, "are oppressing women." I was likened to Hitler; they called me the Great Murderess. But Jesus loves me. I, too, can be saved. Woman against woman, but God was on their side. They were saving babies. They were saving America from the national sin of abortion. The Antis tried to make the word "choice" a word of shame: choice means "death." Choice means "murder." Choice is all evil rolled into a word. Their Orwellian rhetoric tried to obscure the reality: no one wants an abortion. It's not as if someone gets up on a Saturday and says "I think I'll have an abortion today"; it is a situational act of necessity and survival.

The archbishop of New York once likened abortion to the Nazi Holocaust, a distinct analogy—Jews and fetuses. They had to liken fetuses to other known victims to give them personality, to make them more attractive as victims because women's voices didn't count. Women don't count! Southern Baptists once denied women the ability to become priests because they held women "responsible for bringing sin into the world."

There are secular anti-abortionists, too, represented by figures such as the late progressive journalist Nat Hentoff and groups like Secular Pro-Life, which advances the idea that "Life begins at fertilization. . . . [T]he zygote is the first developmental stage of a human being's life cycle. This is not a religious premise; it is a biological fact, attested to in countless biology and embryology texts and affirmed by the majority of biologists worldwide." Such arguments must be developed and used strategically, as the secular anti-abortionists are seen to stand purely on biology. This secular view can serve as the grounds for progressives and "leftists" to take up the anti-abortion cause. If one considers that liberalism or enlightenment progressive thinking is expansive—that is, that it grows philosophically and operationally to include all those who are "othered" in society—then the next group worthy of protection, attention, and vigilant advocacy is fetuses!

One only has to observe the large posters outside of Choices that the Antis put up—for the patients' "education"—to see this visually. There is the ubiquitous image of an open door to a crematorium in Auschwitz with skeletons of Jews hanging out. Then the infamous Jim Crow-era image of a Black man being lynched with white men looking straight into the camera, smiling and smoking. And finally, an image of a large fetus, bloody and torn apart.

The connection is clear: Jews were considered vermin—disease-bearing rodents that were contaminating the body politic of Aryan Germans and as such had to be annihilated. Lynching was the bread and circuses of the day during Jim Crow. And then there are the poor, "innocent" fetuses. They are also not considered human. They are therefore dispensable, open to annihilation and genocide. What's wrong with this picture? What's wrong is that the woman—the individual, grown, reasoning human being that hosts this fetus—is nowhere to be found in this analogy.

With such hateful, violent rhetoric, it was only a matter of time before the protests and the harassment of patients, clinics, and providers gave way to violence, murder, and terror. In Virginia, early one February morning in 1983, seven pipe bombs exploded at the Hillcrest Clinic, which had already been seriously damaged by fire; in Dover, Delaware, in January, arson damaged the Reproductive Care Center; in Prince George's County, Maryland, bombing closed the clinic temporarily with $80,000 worth of damage; in Florida, two clinics were riddled with bullets.

Everywhere was violence, intimidation. Picketing outside the homes of physicians and staff; automobiles smashed and defaced; clinic staffs were afraid to open the mail because of the potential threat of letter bombs; Right to Lifers with cameras outside clinics snapped pictures of all who entered; they took the numbers of license plates, followed cars into clinic parking lots, pouncing on the women as they opened doors and brandishing pictures of bloody fetuses.

Since the Antis had not been able to stop legalized abortion and had not gotten constitutional or legislative change, they had taken matters into their own hands and out into the streets. The Clinic Defense Project compiled statistics: In the early 1980s, the total number of reported incidents at abortion clinics in this country—including picketing, harassment, and violence—rose from 39 in 1982 to 123 in 1983. By March 8, 1984, 59 incidents had already been recorded. In the first half of that decade alone, the estimated cost of damage done by arson to clinics was well over $1 million.

Little has changed over the last four decades. According to the National Abortion Federation's most recent annual Violence and Disruption Statistics report, "many anti-abortion extremists shifted their attention to protective states after dozens of clinics were forced to close in states that banned abortion. Clinics in protective states saw a disproportionate increase in violence and disruption in 2023: Stalking increased by 913 percent (from 8 in 2021 to 81 in 2022); obstructions increased 538 percent (from 45 in 2021 to 287 in 2022); bomb threats increased by 133 percent (from 3 in 2021 to 7 in 2022); burglaries increased by 100 percent (from 5 in 2021 to 10 in 2022); assault and batteries increased by 29 percent (from 7 in 2021 to 9 in 2022)." The report also states that "since 1977, there have been 11 murders, 42 bombings, 200 arsons, 531 assaults, 492 clinic invasions, 375 burglaries, and thousands of other incidents of criminal activities directed at patients, providers, and volunteers."[19]

---

19 "NAF 2022 Violence & Disruption Statistics," National Abortion Federation, 2022, https://prochoice.org/our-work/provider-security/2022-naf-violence-disruption/.

Praise the Lord and Kill the Doctors: Gunn, Tiller, Patterson, Britton

In March 1993, Dr. David Gunn was shot three times in the back by rabid Anti Michael Griffin as he was leaving a Pensacola, Florida, abortion clinic. As soon as I heard that the National Coalition of Abortion Providers was arranging a one-year memorial service in Gunn's memory, I knew I had to be there.

I had never met David, but I had met his brother. One week after his murder, we shared a platform on the Montel Williams show along with John Burt, the former Ku Klux Klan member turned born-again anti-abortionist. Burt was the leader of Advocates for Life Ministries, the radical "pro-life" group that Michael Griffin had joined shortly before he murdered Gunn. I remember the disgust I swallowed listening to his rhetoric about how physicians who performed abortions were murderers, and that stopping them by any means possible was justifiable homicide.

I felt for David's brother, who had chosen to put himself in the position of answering those charges publicly, as if there were some objective reality to them, as if it were necessary to defend a physician who traveled hundreds of miles each week to provide access to abortion services to women who would otherwise have none. But by the immutable laws of television, Williams was intent on giving everyone equal time to "debate."

I knew that by going to Pensacola I was going into enemy territory. There had been a rash of clinic bombings, and the radical fringe of the anti-abortion movement was particularly active in the area. My personal safety was not an issue. I was used to living in a war zone; my own clinic has been picketed repeatedly and I had received a number of death threats during the two decades that I served as director of Choices.

I was surprised, however, when Ellie Smeal, president of the Feminist Majority Foundation, got on the plane with me and after a quick hello told me sotto voce that Paul Hill, the notorious anti-abortion activist, had been sighted at our hotel with two unknown aides. An anonymous threat had been made the night before on television by a man whose face was covered by a large blue dot; we could expect a mass murder, he predicted—something so big that it would surprise both sides—something like Hebron or Beirut.

As if this were not enough, word came down that the FBI had intercepted someone in a car loaded with a cache of weapons, including explosives, headed for the hotel where we were all to stay. Now, this was a little more than even I was used to.

Upon arriving at the hotel, I was told that people planning to attend the memorial were on "high alert." They were aware that threats had been made, and the rumors surrounding the capture of the loaded car made everyone a bit edgy. I subsequently learned that agents in Houston, Texas, had arrested a local anti-abortion activist, Daniel Ware, on weapons charges. At his arraignment, evidence was presented to show that Ware had gone to Pensacola armed with explosives (as well as three guns, one .357 Magnum, and about 2,500 rounds of ammunition) with the stated intention of staging a Beirut-style suicide attack on the abortion providers gathered there.

At the hotel that afternoon the question of whether to go to the memorial service became an "issue" for the providers. Arrangements had been made for most of us to go to the service in buses, yet many felt that would make us moving targets. However, there would be no question of "innocent bystanders" being at risk—something that might give the right-wing Christian terrorists pause. Everyone in the bus would be considered "hardcore" pro-choicers. The police had been notified and we were told that we could expect a full armed escort all the way to the service.

The morning of the memorial a special meeting was called to discuss defensive strategy. It was agreed that a decision not to go would be respected. Many people were frightened. Stronger even than their fear was the bold fact that by not going to the memorial they would be giving in to the terrorists—whose greatest weapon is fear. No one stayed away.

It was sunny and warm when we left for the memorial. But the weather was no balm for the soul, for stationed outside the hotel were armed police, members of the FBI, and the Bureau of Alcohol, Tobacco, and Firearms. The reality of driving to a memorial service for a murdered gynecologist in a procession interspersed with motorcycle cops and police cars was one of the more surreal experiences of my life.

The service was held in an amphitheater opposite the clinic. Given the weather, I was surprised to see Smeal wearing a turtleneck sweater along with a long, dark blue raincoat. Only after a few minutes of looking at her carefully and noticing that she looked rather "boxy" did it occur to me that she was wearing a bullet-proof vest. She was not the only one; two male physicians were outfitted with vests, but they were making no secret of it.

Smeal, however, was almost apologetic. She mentioned more than once that she was wearing it because her son was worried about her and had insisted on it. I thought it interesting that a feminist leader felt it necessary to make an excuse for protecting herself in a dangerous situation—she was "doing it for her children," not herself. The men, however, had no such sensibilities. They did not have to apologize to anyone: they wore their macho on their bulletproof chests. One, in fact, walked within twenty feet of a lone picketer holding a sign that read [sic]: THE WAGES OF SIN IS DEATH and ABORTION IS MURDER. Everyone watched as the doctor pounded his chest and screamed, "Why don't you just do it! Come and get me! You don't have the guts." During this display of righteous passion and provocation, Smeal and I stood next to each other, scanning the tops of buildings for snipers.

This lone picketer, the "Reverend" Paul Hill, described by *The Washington Post* as an anti-abortion "crusader," would later go on to pump three shotgun blasts into the head of Dr. John Bayard Britton on July 29, 1994, in Pensacola, Florida, killing both him and his clinic escort James Barrett and wounding Barrett's wife June.

The service was intense and moving. Gunn's son, just twenty-three, spoke of his pain and loss and pride. A condolence message from President Clinton was read; he wrote of rededicating "ourselves to strengthening the freedoms of choice and privacy," but I thought the words rang hollow. Even with more governmental legislative and popular support for pro-choice policies, the difficulties in providing abortion services had been growing.

A survey by the Feminist Majority had revealed that 50.2 percent of clinics experienced severe anti-abortion violence in the first seven months of that year. Clinics and health care workers faced death threats, stalkers, chemical attacks, arson, bomb threats, invasions, and blockades. Physicians who performed abortions said that they were increasingly outcasts in their profession. There had been a steady decline in abortion training for medical students in the previous six years. Fewer than 12 percent of medical schools were providing first-trimester abortion instruction as part of the required curriculum. That was why Dr. David Gunn had to travel; he was the only abortion provider available within a few hundred miles of his clinic.

It is worth wondering, too, how, in the post-*Dobbs* world, we will train the next generation of providers. According to a study done by Stanford University in 2020—even before *Dobbs*— roughly "half of all medical schools offered no formal abortion training or only a single lecture."[20] The post-*Dobbs* picture is even more grim. At Choices, three of my physicians are at least seventy years old. While we have agreements with major New York hospitals to work with and train their residents, what we lay down now in terms of our core commitment to the work and to its continuance must hold for many future generations.

After Gunn's service, a few of us went to lunch at a local restaurant. In the ladies' room, I watched with amazement, their children in their Sunday best, as Ellie Smeal nonchalantly ripped off her raincoat and sweater to reveal the heavy white vest over her bra which she then quickly removed. I had the strong feeling that I was in a parallel universe; one that, unfortunately, I seem to have become more at home in than the so-called "real one."

I've had this feeling before, most powerfully in the early days

---

20 Roshan M. Burns and Kate A. Shaw, "Standardizing Abortion Education: What Medical Schools Can Learn from Residency Programs," *National Library of Medicine* (December 2020), Abstract, https://pubmed.ncbi.nlm.nih.gov/32969850/.

of 1988 when Operation Rescue came to New York, and I found myself at 5:00 a.m. facing a few hundred people chained together in front of a clinic on the east side singing "Amazing Grace." Everything was going on around me as if it were a day like any other. People were on their way to work, walking their dogs, eating their breakfasts, except I was living in a war zone.

Here it was happening again. Families were coming into the restaurant for their after-church lunch, their children in their Sunday best; while Smeal and I, like two old soldiers, discussed strategic advantages of various anti-terrorist initiatives and exchanged battle stories.

Upon my return to New York, I learned that "Shelly" Shannon, an anti-abortion activist, had been convicted of attempted murder in Wichita, Kansas, after she admitted to shooting—though not fatally—Dr. George Tiller the August before.

Tiller was one of the few physicians in the US at the time who specialized in third-trimester abortions, performing them only when the fetus was deformed or the mother's life was in danger. For many years, I referred women to his clinic for difficult therapeutic late-term abortions, and each of us have shared in subsidizing a young girl's travel, hotel, and medical bills because George was her last and only chance for an abortion. Some months before he was shot, he told me that he always wore a bulletproof vest, and that he drove to work in an armored car.

Shannon, it would appear, had a role model for murder. Copies of letters she sent to Dunn's murderer Michael Griffin while he was in jail awaiting trial praised him as a "hero of our time." She wrote, "I know you did the right thing. It was not murder. I believe in you and what you did." After she learned that Tiller, whom she shot in both arms, had survived the attack, Shannon considered resorting to explosives to blow up his clinic.

In Alabama, a Roman Catholic priest, Rev. David C. Trosch, tried to place an ad in the *Mobile Register* that endorsed the killing of doctors. The ad shows a man pointing a gun at a doctor who is holding a knife over a pregnant woman. Two words accompany the picture: JUSTIFIABLE HOMICIDE.

Two days after the Tiller shooting, Dr. G. Wayne Patterson, owner of six abortion clinics and one of the few physicians to perform abortions in the Mobile/Pensacola area, was killed as he returned to his car in the nightclub district of Mobile. Police attribute his murder to a robbery gone awry, but reports reveal that nothing was stolen from Patterson; his body was left with his wallet on it. Dr. Patterson was a partner of Dr. David Gunn; he owned the clinic at which Gunn was murdered.

Joseph L. Foreman, a Presbyterian minister who helped found Operation Rescue, once wrote: "The transcendent question being forced upon the Anti movement is, do you really think this is murder? You know it would be right if your family was defended from murderers by someone using lethal force. Why not a fetus? To say that it's not murder is to buy the line of the abortionists—that the fetus isn't quite as human as a human."

This thinking was not limited to the right. A group called the Seamless Garment placed ads in traditionally "left" magazines like *Mother Jones*, in which they compared the violence of environmental degradation, nuclear war, and capital punishment with abortion.

Language that compares great movements for social justice with the anti-abortion cause and militant rhetoric that praises murderers, and calls clinics "abortuaries" and their doctors "child slaughterers," created an environment that all but fertilized terrorism. Murderers began to see themselves as saints. "Is it really so bad?" Shannon was quoted after the killing of Dr. Gunn. "People cheered when Hitler was killed, and the abortionist was a mass murderer."

Dallas Blanchard, author of *Religious Violence and Abortion*, studied the profiles of those arrested for violent acts against clinics. They are split, he said, between long-time activists frustrated at their lack of success and those with only a short-term involvement in the movement who are hungry for celebrity or martyrdom. "I think the violence in the future will continue to come from both directions," Blanchard predicted. "The dam has a hole in it now."

This "hole" was filled to some extent by a Supreme Court ruling that allowed abortion clinics to invoke the federal racketeering law in suing violent anti-abortion groups for damages. The FACE Act—Federal Access to Clinic Entrances—which makes it a federal offense to block people's access to clinics helped, too. But they were not enough. For terrorists who believe they are doing "God's work," the laws of the state are mere obstacles on the road to salvation.

In 2020, a group of anti-abortion protesters established a blockade outside a clinic in Washington, DC, and opened a new legal theater of war. The case is now being reviewed by a US District Court to determine whether the protesters violated the FACE Act. If convicted, the women face a maximum sentence of eleven years in prison, three years of supervised release, and a fine of up to $350,000. Additionally, the case could have lasting effects, further hampering the opposition from taking extreme measures. However, because of the intensity and commitment of the opposing sides, the court struggled to find an impartial jury to hear the case.

"*Dobbs* is the law, Roe is gone, and yet there's still no nation-wide ban on abortion. . . . that impulse to take the law into one's own hands may be strong right now," said Mary Ziegler, a legal historian of the anti-abortion movement at the University of California at Davis.

Nothing, ultimately, could save Dr. Tiller. On May 31, 2009, sixteen years after surviving one attempted murder, he was fatally shot in the head by anti-abortion extremist Scott Roeder on a Sunday, when Tiller was acting as deacon in his church in Wichita, Kansas. Vicious and terrifying as it was, there was a method to their madness. They knew that without providers there is no such thing as choice; legal abortion is merely theoretical if there is no one willing and technically capable of doing the procedure. Many of the early physicians, whose commitment was formed by the experience of having women die in their arms or in hospital emergency rooms from botched abortions, have died or retired. The increasing number of physicians unwilling to perform the procedure because of harassment, or lack of commitment and the dearth of medical schools willing to train residents, resulted in the need for traveling doctors like David Gunn.

George Tiller was a friend, colleague, and associate of mine for over a quarter of a century. I shared time and ideas with him at conferences. I referred patients for his services and exchanged holiday gifts with his staff. He, like so many abortion providers, was a person of courage, integrity, and commitment to women's reproductive rights. I was sobered and deeply saddened by his murder, but not surprised. Facing ongoing legal and violent harassment, he continued to work for women on a daily basis in the middle of this war zone that all providers share. George lived on that line, defended it, and paid with his life. I am profoundly grateful for that life, lived with conviction and honor.

Joseph Campbell, in *The Hero with a Thousand Faces*, believes that everyone faces heroic opportunities. In a sense, one could say that heroes are defined not so much by their position in life as by their attitude toward it, a stance of active engagement. Although Campbell writes of an ageless heroic myth that has universal application in all cultures, the hero in America has come to be synonymous with the "great man." He, as hero, is the avatar of humanity who encompasses a transcendent value, such as courage or loyalty, and, ideally, puts his life at extreme risk for the good of others or of the whole community. By this definition, one could reasonably argue that women and girls are by their very nature heroic. The physical risks they face are global and transgenerational—the risk of pregnancy, abortion, rape, childbirth, intimate violence, oppression—risks that for the most part are faced for their husbands, children, and others that make up their community. However, these are unchosen risks, the ones that come with the territory of being female. They do not belong to the style of risk that is usually labeled heroic.

Courage has been called the prime virtue because one acts in spite of one's fears. Courage is not a lack of fear but controlling it. My childhood fantasies and heroes always "assumed" my courage. I challenged a great evil power. I was forced to protect and defend my land, my people, my principles. Of course, however great the odds were against me, I always triumphed. Like Wonder Woman with her magic weapons, I always remained physically untouched and forever invincible. Oddly enough, my dreams have not died, nor have I outgrown my need for them. Quite the contrary. They have formed a psychological background that has subtly merged with my political and personal landscape. As president of Choices, my warrior fantasies took on a definitively realistic tone. There are positions and staff to defend, and women to protect against invasions from both the anti-abortionists and their own unwanted pregnancies. The risks have become so real that my life sometimes feels like one of those Shakespearean plays performed in modern dress, with shotguns instead of swords and T-shirts instead of tunics.

Where Were My Troops?

The threats following Dr. Gunn's murder had pushed me into buying my first shotgun, a twenty-gauge, pump-action Mossberg—an action reported on page 6 of the *New York Post* under the column head "Make Her Day."

Explaining that the gun was bought for protection in my country house, I said, "If you're looking for violence, it's the anti-choice people who harass and hunt people down." The image of me challenging the Antis to "draw" was more prophetic than comical, and in the days to come I would think deeply about the nature of the cause I would die, kill, or be killed for.

Within two days of Dr. Britton's death, Choices received three bomb threats and a phone call saying, "I have a gun and will be hunting your doctors next week." Although Choices had received many bomb threats since it opened, and I receive death threats on a continual basis (particularly around Easter, Christmas, and Mother's Day), this time it felt different.

Frantically, my mother kept calling from Florida asking me why I insisted on going into the clinic. I explained to her I was not living a normal life and that the situation demanded courage and engagement, not retreat.

But I knew that I was a lightning rod and a high-profile target. This time, I thought, they might really kill me or my staff. I felt a combination of anxiety and intense energy; I was in battle, and I was in character.

During this era of heightened clinic violence, Choices had a 115-person staff, including seven doctors, and was seeing almost a thousand patients a week, about three hundred of which were for abortions. The other visits were for things like prenatal care, counseling, birth control, and all general gynecological care. Understandably, our staff was upset and anxious. The doctors discussed wearing bulletproof vests, but stopped when they recalled that Dr. Britton was wearing one when he was blasted in the head.

"Perhaps I should come to work in a full suit of armor," one doctor joked nervously.

The ironic part was that Dr. Britton's murder took place only two months after the Federal Access to Clinic Entrances (FACE) Act had been signed into law by President Clinton. For years, anti-abortion violence and harassment against clinic patients and staff were not taken seriously by the law enforcement community.

Protecting clinics and their staff and patients was not a high priority. We had turned into sitting ducks. Women had been putting their lives on the line for years—and often losing them—in the struggle for abortion rights. Yet, it was only after Dr. Gunn (a man) had been killed in the battle that the law-enforcement establishment became involved.

Where were my troops? I wondered. Although Choices had a group of loyal clinic escorts who were on duty every Saturday morning to counteract the Antis' harassment of patients, they were a meager substitute for twelve-gauge shotguns.[21] I had no armed throng of supporters defending my gates in the days after Dr. Britton's death. What I did do was reinforce, with armed guards, internal security procedures honed after years of dealing with bomb threats and potential invasions from Operation Rescue. Then I found out about Henry Felisone and Tony Piso.

These two New York City residents had signed Paul Hill's infamous petition describing the "use of lethal force in the killing of

---

21 The volunteer group providing clinic escorts at Choices was originally organized by Choices and NOW (National Organization of Women). They have grown to almost 200 members and publish their own newsletter, train other groups of escorts, and have made a courageous and continual stand against the harassment by the Antis.

Dr. David Gunn as justifiable, provided it was carried out for the purpose of defending the lives of unborn children." And they lived within a ten-block radius of Choices.

The danger was clear and present. Federal protection had been ordered for other clinics under siege around the country, and my staff needed visible signs of support. I called the New York State attorney general, demanding protection. Two days later, Washington acted, and two federal marshals were posted in front of Choices on a twenty-four-hour basis. "These people are terrorists and should be picked up for just making threats," I told the *New York Post*.

The FBI agents who were investigating the threats to Choices were new to the intricacies of the FACE Act and were unsure about jurisdictional issues.

I found myself in the strange position of having to coordinate representatives of the civil rights and criminal divisions of the FBI with my local police precinct to begin an investigation of Felisone and Piso on criminal conspiracy charges.

It wasn't until after the murder of Britton, the second doctor to die in nineteen months, that government officials seriously began to consider and investigate the possibility of an organized national anti-abortion conspiracy to kill providers. I believed it was a serious strategic mistake to view the murders of the two doctors as acts of individual madness. The evidence can be extracted from both the statements of anti-abortionists about what to expect in the way of more killings and the intellectual climate that has been, I believe, deliberately created to undermine support for freedom of choice—even among its strongest proponents.

Consider the words of Don Treshman, director of Rescue America, who was quoted in *The New York Times* saying that Dr. Britton's killing "may be the start of a new civil war." He continued, "Up to now, the killings have been on one side, with thirty million dead babies and hundreds of dead and maimed mothers. On the other side, there are two dead doctors. Maybe the balance is going to start to shift."

The first time I heard the Civil War analogy used to describe the abortion struggle was in 1983 when I debated Nellie Gray, an anti-abortion leader who helped coordinate the yearly January 22 right-to-life march on Washington. During a break in our taping, she told me, "You know, this is just like the Lincoln-Douglas debates on slavery," casting herself as Abraham Lincoln. Of course, she did not seem to consider bearing a child against one's will as a special form of slavery. Given that there has been an "open season" on providers for years, positioning the abortion struggle as a civil war—or any type of war—is basically optimistic. The guns are all on one side, and women, regardless of which side they may fall on, are most often the casualties. I would call this a *war of aggression* and *gender genocide*.

Years of anti-choice rhetoric positioning abortionists as murderers and clinics as "abortoriums" were the metaphorical gun; it just needed the real bullets. True believers concluded that killing doctors was working for Christ and their own salvation. The fetuses are "innocent" and must be protected at all costs against the barbarian hordes who so casually annihilate them. In this situation, these anti-abortion "crusaders" are slashing and burning their way to God's city on the hill, killing the infidels in their path. God's word was the theory. Killing doctors, bombing clinics, and harassing women was the practice.

Holding the "moral" white banner in defense of "innocent human life" as a positive value in comparison with the "pro-death" forces who allow women the right to control their own bodies places the issue in a context where people like the Reverend Trosch can tell *The New York Times* that it would not trouble his conscience if he learned that someone had actually killed an abortion doctor: "You're comparing the lives of morally guilty persons against the lives of manifestly innocent persons." Moral innocence is reflexively considered an absolute good. It is something that we think of in terms of losing. But can innocence be active? And in the case of the fetus, how does the label of innocence translate and codify into a being whose rights can actually trump a full-reasoning living woman's?

Writing in *The Hill*, Lloyd Steffen, a professor of religious studies and university chaplain, posits:

> To offer innocence as a reason for fetal supremacy is not the same as saying that protections for the fetus flow from species membership—the fact that the fetus is human. Of course, it is—a human conceptus is not a frog—but we make all kinds of exceptions to allow for actions that bring about the end of human life, everything from self-defense and permissible losses of non-combatants in warfare to the cessation of life support for brain dead patients. The absolute value of fetal life has been most prominently advanced in Roman Catholic moral teaching, but the church also preserved in Western culture the just war tradition, a perspective that opposes war but allows for exceptions in certain specified situations if certain justice criteria are met. Although this mode of moral analysis focuses on possible exceptions to generally held moral positions, the Catholic moral tradition does not apply this ethic to the fetus and to abortion. That is because, in the words of John Paul II, the fetus is not only innocent but *"absolutely innocent."*
>
> With abortion, the pope wrote, "we are dealing with murder." Regarding the fetus, "No one more absolutely innocent could be imagined." And the pope denied that a life-threatening medical problem could render abortion an act of self-defense, declaring, "In no way could this human being ever be considered an aggressor, much less an unjust aggressor.[22]

So, one can see why the very idea that a woman can define a fetus growing in her body as an unwanted aggressor—as a kind of metastasis—would be the ultimate negation of the Christian view of God and reality. And the horror that so many feel when reading about the cruelty as a result of *Dobbs*—stories like that of the mother in Florida who was denied an abortion after her

22 Lloyd Steffen, "The Misleading Question of Innocence Distorts the Abortion Debate," *The Hill*, June 26, 2022, https://thehill.com/opinion/judiciary/3534690-the-misplaced-question-of-innocence-distorts-the-abortion-debate/.

baby's fatal diagnosis and was forced to give birth to a baby that lived only ninety-nine minutes—simply does not resonate for the true believers. For them there are no "just wars" in abortion—no self-defense—only the condemnation of those who would willingly slaughter these *absolute* innocents.

The Sanctity of Life

I have never shied away from the fact and the reality that abortion is an act of terminating potential or ongoing or growing human life. It is not just blood and tissue, which is what pro-choice forces will argue to minimize the argument on the anti-choice side. The Antis will argue for the sanctity of life. But we must see the hypocrisy when the concept of the "sanctity of life" can be totally redefined in situations where it is the state providing the definition, such as with *Dobbs*. The Antis will always push for a total ban on abortion and toward a redefinition of the fetus as a person with rights. Many Antis are comfortable supporting capital punishment and opposing abortion, because they are not really talking about the sanctity of life, but the sanctity of *innocent* life.

A few days after the murder of Dr. Britton, Cardinal O'Connor of New York, who had recently appeared on the front page of the *New York Post* threatening to go to jail in an act of civil disobedience if abortion was included in a national health-care package, issued a passionate statement to *The New York Times* on August 6.

"If anyone has an urge to kill an abortionist, let him kill me instead. That's about as clearly as I can renounce such madness," the cardinal proclaimed. The fact that O'Connor had deflected a bullet to himself rather than disarming his anti-choice rhetoric was in character. He was not condemning violence per se, merely asking for a change of venue. Meanwhile, what we got from the media was the kind of sports mentality that views everything in neatly competitive categories: right to life 2; pro-choice 0. Cable channel New York 1, for example, wanted me to "debate" two Antis on the "issue" of whether or not murdering doctors was "justifiable homicide." I declined, telling them that this was like asking the SS guards at Auschwitz to debate the inmates on the "issue" of the efficacy of genocide by gas inhalation.

Paul Hill had used the media to defend his position on the justification of murdering doctors who perform abortions. "We're saying thirty million children have died. Sometimes you have to use force to stop people from killing innocent children," he told *Nightline*. Two days after Gunn's murder, Hill called the *Donahue* show to set up an appearance to announce that Dr. Gunn deserved to die.

Another perhaps even more dangerous casualty of the relentless onslaught on abortion and abortion providers was to increase a sense of ambivalence about abortion itself as a moral or necessary choice. Many people who describe themselves as politically pro-choice and are committed theoretically to the issue often feel the need to say, "I don't like abortion, but . . ."

Unappreciated and unrecognized, viewed as mavericks at best or outcasts at worst by establishment institutional medicine, abortion providers stood alone, apart and vulnerable. For historical and political reasons, most abortion services are performed at outpatient, freestanding facilities. Risking their lives on an almost daily basis, doctors and other health care workers continue to provide services in a war zone where only one side is armed.

The casualties *continue* to mount and again I ask: Where are my troops?

CHAPTER 5
ROE OVERTURNED

A State of Total War

I did many interviews in the days after the *Dobbs* decision. Reporters had been following me around, and they wanted to know what I was thinking. I knew the impact of the decision would be felt around the world and I knew many of the interviews would be going out internationally. My message was simple. It was the same message I had delivered to my staff: Yes, this is terrible. Yes, this is appalling. We can mourn. We can look at how we got here. But we *have* to organize, we have to fight, and we have to change it. It brought me back to my house burning down: It's gone; now it's time to rebuild.

It took about one month for a lot of the other pro-choice organizations to move on from "I understand your pain" and setting up support groups on social media. It was an orgy of emotion. It made me angry. I wanted to shout: *You think freedom is free? You think you don't have to be vigilant?* My thinking after *Dobbs* was that we needed to get over it and get on with it—to get into the streets and fight. That sense of mourning has to be turned into righteous rage. When I read stories of the personal suffering that this decision will mean for women, I can't stand it. I feel a kind of anger that if unbridled would overwhelm me, but also despair and sadness over the evil and cruelty in this world.

If you are not feeling some kind of rage or despair, you are not awake. I don't mean "woke." I mean awake to the reality of the world. I am very awake to it. I live in it. I'm grateful that I can channel those feelings and, with a sliver of hope, try to make a difference. I consider that a gift and a responsibility. When you live in a reality like mine, there is no time for filters, no room for solidified perceptions. There is only the pure energy necessary to continue fighting. Conflict exists on every level: between the state and the individual; between us and the opposition; even within the women themselves—intimate wars—and it is always a war for survival. And power.

As a result of my work at the clinic, I was living in this state of total war long before *Roe* was overturned. Lawsuits, invasions, bomb threats, and death threats have plagued me for decades. The question is how to keep going. Unlike the Antis, most in the prochoice movement don't have God above them saying, "You will be redeemed, you are doing my work, you are saving babies, this is part of my plan."

What we do have is a deep belief in the concept of individual women's moral freedom in terms of Reproductive Justice, and the necessity to ensure that this is recognized nationally in a legal, constitutional, or legislative form that cannot be undone. Those like me who have had decades of experience with millions of women making these decisions can attest that the state (or states) have no right to qualify this. The power of the state must stop at our skin! What I do have is my profound belief in the truth as I have experienced it with over a million women. I have no choice but to fight.

Anti Propaganda and the Weaponization of Religion

The Antis have been extremely effective in their propaganda efforts to create shame, stigma, and guilt around abortion. They have convinced so many people of a narrative that says abortion is evil, that it is the killing of an unborn child, that there is something wrong with the women seeking abortions. They didn't make the right choice. They couldn't keep their legs closed. They aren't "good" girls.

Deciding to have an abortion is never an easy thing. It can be a very emotional time for the patient and often for her escort or partner, especially when we have to talk them down from the people outside screaming at them "you're going to burn in hell!" and in a high-pitched voice "Mommy, please don't murder me." Individuals, particularly those in stressful situations or experiencing heightened emotional states, are very susceptible to the loaded arguments and misinformation surrounding abortion. Combine this with the demonstrators outside the clinics screaming and yelling that these women are "killing their babies" (and offering them water because they know if they have a drink, they will not be able to have general anesthesia), and the result can be emotionally toxic.

Recognizing the problem, in 2017, former New York attorney general Eric Schneiderman went so far as to file a lawsuit against the anti-choice protestors over the harassment that was going on outside of Choices. I thought back to the times that Bishop Daily, bishop of Brooklyn and Queens, would lead hundreds of his parishioners to our front doors in "prayer vigils." There they would stand—rosaries in hand, bouquets of flowers held up to the sky in gentle supplication—singing "Amazing Grace" and praying for my soul and the souls of the "murdered unborn" inside my clinic. I would find myself at times mentally singing along with them, feeling the sweet ache of guilt and assumed forgiveness, the giving up of oneself, the primal and profound desire for that unconditional love.

"The tactics used to harass and menace Choices' patients, families, volunteers, and staff are not only horrifying—they're illegal," said Schneiderman. "The law guarantees women the right to control their own bodies and access the reproductive health care they need, without obstruction. We'll do what it takes to protect those rights for women across New York."

According to the attorney general's press release, "these protestors descend on approaching patients, sometimes walking them into the clinic's exterior wall and pinning them against it. Protestors are alleged to crowd patients arriving by car, using their bodies to block the passenger-side doors and thrust their heads and hands through any open windows. Protestors are also alleged to deliberately collide into the volunteer escorts, and sometimes push and shove them, as the escorts try to shield patients from this unwanted physical contact and vitriol. These anti-choice protestors are also alleged to make violent threats against both the escorts and patients, referring to terrorist attacks and murderous assaults on abortion clinics, and warning that the same fate may befall them. These obstructive tactics routinely deter or delay patients who are attempting to access medically necessary care, as detailed in the Attorney General's lawsuit."[23]

Ultimately, the district court judge—a Republican and Trump appointee—sided with the protestors, who claimed they did not harass patients and were "only preaching God's word," and refused to file the injunction. After losing two appeals, Schneiderman's successor dropped the lawsuit and the protesters' lawyers called it "a great victory."

The stigma and shame attached to abortion is truly extraordinary. Which is why I speak and write so much about coming out of the abortion closet and being able to own your decision. We must be able to say "I had an abortion. I made that moral choice." Remember, traditionally, abortion was not a religious issue. It had been, rather, a scientific and medical issue. As Randall Balmer, the John Phillips Professor in Religion at Dartmouth College and the author of *Bad Faith: Race and the Rise of the Religious Right,* wrote in *Politico*: "White evangelicals in the 1970s did not mobilize against *Roe v. Wade,* which they considered a Catholic issue. . . . To suggest otherwise is to perpetuate what I call the abortion myth, the fiction that the genesis of the Religious Right—the powerful evangelical political movement that has reshaped American politics over the past four decades—lay in opposition to abortion." Balmer continues:

---

23 "A.G. Schneiderman Files Lawsuit To End Persistent Harassment Of Women Entering Women's Health Clinic In Queens," Office of the New York State Attorney General, https://ag.ny.gov/press-release/2017/ag-schneiderman-files-lawsuit-end -persistent-harassment-women-entering-womens.

When Francis Schaeffer, the intellectual godfather of the Religious Right, tried to enlist Billy Graham in his antiabortion crusade in the late 1970s, Graham, the most famous evangelical of the twentieth century, turned him down. Even James Dobson, founder of Focus on the Family who later became an implacable foe of abortion, acknowledged in 1973 that the Bible was silent on the matter and therefore it was plausible for an evangelical to believe that "a developing embryo or fetus was not regarded as a full human being."[24]

There are, of course, religious people who deeply support a woman's right to choose. Catholics for Free Choice has been a leader in the struggle. Their former president, Fran Kissling, with whom I founded the National Abortion Federation (NAF), has long been an intellectual and theoretical bridge for articulating how abortion should be incorporated into the Catholic belief system.

But people find Jesus in the strangest of places. He seems to relish coming in chance epiphanies, catching folks unexpected and amazed. So, when news broke that Norma McCorvey, aka Jane Roe of *Roe v. Wade*, the "poster girl for choice," had gotten herself baptized in a Florida swimming pool by a leader of Operation Rescue, I was not surprised. Reverend Flip Benham, who did the honors, reported that Jesus Christ "had reached through the abortion mill wall and touched the heart of Norma McCorvey." According to Benham, Norma found Jesus "at the gates of Hell."

During my years at Choices, I have heard many firsthand reports about Jesus. It is not unusual for women to recount their private dialogues with him as they lie prepped for their abortions or wake drowsy and vulnerable from anesthesia.

"I just know he understands," they will say. "I believe he will forgive me."

"He wants me to be able to care for the two children I have."

"God is love, isn't he?"

---

24 Randall Balmer, "The Religious Right and the Abortion Myth, *Politico*, May 10, 2022, https://www.politico.com/news/magazine/2022/05/10/abortion-history-right -white-evangelical-1970s-00031480.

Misogyny Dressed as Religion

As I stated earlier, abortion only really came onto the political scene after the fall of communism, when another enemy was needed. With communism out of the way, the right effectively weaponized the religious context in which abortion is often considered. It was a gateway issue, and they were able to appeal to a large number of otherwise non-political constituents. Recall that Reagan was a pro-choice governor, who later switched when it became politically convenient to do so. Bush was pro-choice and he switched. They saw that they could activate a major evangelical voting block by talking about and opposing abortion rights. It was red meat, so to speak.

Looking through realistic (i.e. cynical) eyes, this was little more than desire for political power merged with generic misogyny masquerading as religious morality. They used the authority of the church to codify—and then *sanctify*—anti-abortion positions. At a certain point it was no longer one group's religious conviction, it was the word of God. But it is nothing more than religion being weaponized in order to control women. You can see this across the timeline, from the earliest pollsters like Ralph Reed, a political consultant and first executive director of the Christian Coalition in the nineties, to people like Jerry Falwell, a Baptist pastor well-known for founding the Moral Majority, which was on its way to becoming one of the largest lobby groups for evangelical Christians in the country.

In the early 1980s, I was asked to fly to Detroit to debate Reverend Falwell. I believe it was the first time he had to debate anyone from "my side." I had absolutely no major non-profit organizational affiliation. I only had Choices. I was the devil incarnate. At one point in the debate, he looked at me and said, "Ms. Hoffman, how many abortions did your facility do last year?"

"Nine thousand, Reverend," I answered.

"Nine thousand!" he shouted. "Nine thousand. How will you meet your maker with the blood of nine thousand babies on your hands?"

"When I meet Her," I said, "I will be very proud, because I fought for women's rights!"

"Her? Her? Are you saying God is a woman?" he asked, a look of total astonishment on his face.

"No, Reverend. I am saying that God is beyond gender."

Despite my efforts on the debate stage, Falwell's popularity continued to surge. As more and more people were brought into megachurches like his, a Republican alliance came naturally. It is not surprising that we ended up with three conversative, anti-abortion Catholics on the Supreme Court. It was the organic evolution of a political party all too happy to use religion to justify its desire to control women. These appointees are all practicing fundamentalists. It is as if they are rejecting the concepts of the Enlightenment—the belief that reason, science, and logic give people more knowledge and understanding of reality than religion. They are, in many ways, doing this to hold the line against the rapid dechristianization going on in this country.

How else to explain the support for someone like Donald Trump, a man who is the very antithesis of so-called Christian values? They value the message over the messenger, and they believe God works in mysterious ways. For people like this, the ends justify the means; having to create or support an evil to prevent a further evil. For example, dropping the bomb on Hiroshima to end the war in the Pacific.

Mahatma Gandhi said, "The means are an end in process." The dystopian reality that *Dobbs* has brought forth is a means whose immediate results are the sacrifice that must be paid for the Ultimate Good of saving innocent babies' lives.

So the casualties of *Roe*, the horror of being forced to carry a child against your will, or having to "bleed out" prior to being able to be admitted for emergency hospital treatment may be horrendous for the individual involved, but the ultimate goal of saving all those babies overrides that.

In a sense, belief itself is a choice. Religious people make a choice to believe. They *take* a "leap of faith." We all have to answer certain questions for ourselves: *Why am I here? What is the meaning of life?* A lot of people believe that traditional religion offers the answers to those questions, and there is no argument that will convince them otherwise. (In a dialogue with Elie Wiesel, I asked him what the meaning of life was. He answered, "You will never know the meaning of life. You have to know the meaning of *your* life.")

Nevertheless, the religious worldview is appealing largely because it answers the unanswerable questions about the real meaning of life—your life in particular. It historically provides a kind of road map of reality. The more complex our world becomes, the more important it becomes to have such a map toward meaning. Otherwise, it's chaos. And what part can one person play in all that chaos?

The issue of abortion goes beyond right and wrong as defined by religions. Atheists can say something is morally wrong or right, but religious people are speaking to a "higher" authority. Many don't believe atheists can even be moral. I believe we can all use reason to guide us toward empathy, compassion, and community—independent of any higher authority. We do not need Falwell saying AIDS is "God's punishment" for abortion in order to live a moral life. Every day, we at Choices bear witness to each woman's realization that she holds the profound power to decide if the potential life within her can come to term. The sharing of those moments makes abortion work, in and of itself, sacred.

Many religious people believe that women will decide not to abort if abortion is illegal. That will not happen. That is not reality. Opponents to legal abortion cannot seem to engage or feel the depth of compassion necessary to understand the results of such a policy. In earlier days, I have debated nearly every leader of the opposition. I understand them. But I can't change the minds of the truly committed. I cannot convince them that the issue of abortion touches very deep chords within *individual* lives, which is, again, why it must be an *individual* decision.

Misinformation

Rather than deepening their sense of compassion and practicing empathy and love, the opposition preys on fear. They put out information that says abortion causes breast cancer, or abortion causes depression. Every legitimate scientific study has shown these to be false facts. (Dr. C. Everett Koop, the surgeon general under President Reagan, angered the Antis when he reviewed the literature and concluded that abortion did not negatively affect mental health.)

No matter how many times they are debunked, they persist. People believe them. There is so much information and misinformation being disseminated now, it can be very difficult to cut through it. I go back to what Joseph Goebbels, Hitler's minister of propaganda, said, which is that if you tell a lie over and over and over again, people will start to believe it. The bigger the lie, the more they will believe. We are living in a post-truth world, and in such an environment, the Antis have grown extremely adept at promoting narratives of guilt and shame based on all kinds of lies and propaganda. It is a cruel but terribly effective strategy.

It is important to be honest about abortion. There has been a debate about when a fetus can feel pain. The scientific consensus was at twenty-four weeks, which is why abortion had been relatively unregulated under *Roe* up to twenty-four weeks. More recent studies have shown that it is possible that the fetus can in fact experience pain earlier. This is a debatable point, and an important debate because it has the potential to impact a woman's abortion decision and affect the surgical techniques that are used in the process. However, what is not debatable is that women can and do feel pain. We can debate the fetal heartbeat, but a woman's heart is beating. There can be no debate about that.

It is, of course, true that a fetus is a living organism and that if you *do not* terminate the pregnancy (and there is no miscarriage—26 percent of all pregnancies end in miscarriage, usually in the first twelve weeks) after nine months, a woman will deliver a baby. So, is abortion killing? Is it, as Dr. Warren Hern (a physician who for decades performed late-term abortions) calls it, "destruction"? I understand, and every woman understands, what it is to terminate a pregnancy. They may not articulate it, they may not want to come out and say it, but they have to narrate, create a "story," and integrate it into their lives in a way they can live with. It is a moral decision. It may not be something a woman must be proud of, but it is something they can and should stand by.

Dobbs and the Clinics

Too often abortion is nothing but a political football, when in reality abortion is the result of an individual's choice, something the government should have minimal if any say in. This is why, for years, I have tried to get as many activists and people involved in the movement as possible to come to Choices—to experience it for themselves. It is often a life-changing experience.

There is a false belief that an abortion clinic is something akin to a drab, depressing, industrialized killing space. When people come to Choices, they meet the staff, see the patients and the moving, educational artwork and design, and most leave profoundly moved. Many people on both sides of the movement claim to be speaking for women, but the providers are the ones on the front lines. It is in the clinics where you can see clearly that abortion is not some legal or theoretical construct—it is real life. Real decisions being wrestled with and made.

Many of the patients are minority women bringing up children on their own. Considering the brutal economic challenges so many of my patients face, I'm amazed by how they do it. I see Choices as an oasis for them. For a short time, they can sit alone with a counselor and talk about how *they* feel. It's a tiny moment, a pebble in a tsunami of what's going on in their lives. But it is important. I want people to see for themselves; to talk to the incredible, committed staff who—when there is a bomb threat—show up the next day. I couldn't do this without them. But the outcast status runs very deep. Some members of my staff have told me they won't tell certain members of their family where they work. I coached them about how to talk to their families about this issue and help them work through the process.

It is worth asking, as the *Washington Post* did in December 2022, why we "rely so heavily on clinics in the first place? Why isn't abortion accessible through the same channels we use for other prescriptions and outpatient procedures? In a country where one in ten women travel out of state to terminate pregnancies *before Dobbs*, why can't doctor's offices and hospitals pick up more of the load?"[25]

When New York legalized abortion in 1970, there was no such thing as an abortion clinic. Because all abortions were surgical at that time, and all "surgeries" were performed in a hospital, the legalization of abortion brought about the birth of the entire ambulatory care movement. Aside from the two large facilities that were doing two to three hundred abortions per day in eight ORs, there were a plethora of doctor's offices that were also doing abortions. The offices would hire staff, rent more space, and call themselves "women's clinics."

Women's clinics were the forerunners of ambulatory health centers. After experiencing how effective freestanding abortion clinics could be in terms of safety, volume, staff, and cost, doctors realized many other procedures were possible outside of the hospitals. Because the health care system is so heavily regulated in New York, any doctor who truly wanted to build and operate a clinic should ideally have sought licensure from the state. But because licensing or building an abortion clinic is a very expensive regulatory procedure, most doctors' offices just continued to operate normally and put themselves out to the public as a "clinic."

---

25 Sarah Green Carmichael, "Abortion Clinics Shouldn't Have to Stand Alone," *Washington Post*, December 16, 2022, https://www.washingtonpost.com/business /abortion-clinics-shouldnt-have-to-stand-alone/2022/12/16/8dcf4032–7d46–11ed -bb97-f47d47466b9a_story.html.

Consumers of abortion services are mostly ignorant of the fact that the state has absolutely no right to regulate anything that is done in a doctor's office. If a doctor decides that she wants to perform a hysterectomy or mastectomy in their office, they can do this without any interference. Only in *licensed* clinics are procedures standardized, staff must have certain credentials, and space must architecturally conform to building codes. So many of the clinics around the country have been forced to close because their state departments of health or the legislatures have passed laws requiring doctors' offices to meet standards of licensed ambulatory surgery facilities.

Knowing the difference between a licensed facility and a "doctor's office," I chose to build Choices as an ambulatory surgery center. I wanted to practice medicine at the highest standards. This is the reason why, when I became the first president of NAF, one of the first things I did was publish a pamphlet called "How to Choose an Abortion Clinic." In my case, the licensed ambulatory clinic structure allowed me to develop an innovative model of care that patients would never find in hospitals. Creativity and feminism could flourish within these walls. Unfortunately, at the same time, we were not only targets of harassment, bombs, and killings by the Antis, we were not embraced or even supported by the hospitals or the medical system.

The hospitals did not want to be "contaminated by abortion," which was seen as toxic. The sentiment was, "We don't do them. Send them somewhere else." Abortion clinics were beyond the pale to many of the medical practitioners.

Long before *Dobbs* came down, the Antis were waging guerrilla warfare on clinics to effectively remove them from the body politic. According to the *Washington Post*: "Data from the abortion care network estimate that the number of independent clinics in the US fell 35 percent over the last ten years. And the pace of closure has doubled in 2022." Closing the clinics is the most egregious result of *Dobbs*, but even if a state's laws allow abortion in some circumstances, the arbitrary obstacles placed on providers and clinics have a strangling effect on providing services. Below are the current numbers on clinical restrictions and requirements. Many of these were in place prior to *Dobbs*:[26]

Physician and Hospital Requirements: 32 states require an abortion to be performed by a licensed physician. 19 states require an abortion to be performed in a hospital after a specified point in the pregnancy, and 17 states require the involvement of a second physician after a specified point.

Gestational Limits: 43 states prohibit abortions after a specified point in pregnancy, with some exceptions provided. The allowable circumstances are generally when an abortion is necessary to protect the patient's life or health.

"Partial-Birth" Abortion: 21 states have laws in effect that prohibit "partial-birth" abortion. 3 of these laws apply only to post-viability abortions.

Public Funding: 16 states use their own funds to pay for all or most medically necessary abortions for Medicaid enrollees in the state. 33 states and the District of Columbia prohibit the use of state funds except in those cases when federal funds are available: where the patient's life is in danger or the pregnancy is the result of rape or incest. In defiance of federal requirements, South Dakota limits funding to cases of life endangerment only.

Coverage by Private Insurance: 12 states restrict coverage of abortion in private insurance plans, most often limiting coverage only to when the patient's life would be endangered if the pregnancy were carried to term. Most states allow the purchase of additional abortion coverage at an additional cost.

Refusal: 45 states allow individual health care providers to refuse to participate in an abortion. 42 states allow institutions to refuse to perform abortions, 16 of which limit refusal to private or religious institutions.

State-Mandated Counseling: 17 states mandate that individuals be given counseling before an abortion that includes information

---

26 "Communities Need Clinics: 2022 Report At-A-Glance," Abortion Care Network, 2022, https://abortioncarenetwork.org/wp-content/uploads/2022/12/CNC-2022-one-pager.pdf.

on at least one of the following: the purported link between abortion and breast cancer (5 states), the ability of a fetus to feel pain (12 states) or long-term mental health consequences for the patient (8 states).

Waiting Periods: 24 states require a person seeking an abortion to wait a specified period of time, usually 24 hours, between when they receive counseling and the procedure is performed. 12 of these states have laws that effectively require the patient make two separate trips to the clinic to obtain the procedure.

Parental Involvement: 36 states require some type of parental involvement in a minor's decision to have an abortion. 27 states require one or both parents to consent to the procedure, while 9 require that one or both parents be notified.

In essence, the Antis pushed for clinics to meet certain regulatory standards which would have cost them millions of dollars. Many of the independent clinics whose revenues came solely from patient services could not afford to stay open. Anything the Antis could do to close them, they did. An organization like Planned Parenthood, which has a long-standing national reputation coupled with many millions of nonprofit dollars, could afford to create advertising and literature, and keep most of their clinics open. This was on the back of competitive practices which included opening their clinics on the same block or very close to a small independent clinic. Think Barnes and Noble opening up right near your local bookstore. Smaller independent clinics simply couldn't survive.

At one point I was compelled to write to Laura McQuade, then the head of Planned Parenthood in New York, to draw her attention to the fact that Planned Parenthood parked an Outreach Bus two blocks from Choices. "Planned Parenthood staff are handing out pamphlets about your services to Choices' potential patients (and perhaps even current patients)—competitively marketing right at my door!" I wrote. "I really can't imagine that you have authorized this—considering we had such a good meeting when you visited Choices a few months ago when I shared so much of my work and Choices with you. However this happened, I am respectfully requesting as a comrade in a war with the Antis (not with each other) that you cease and desist this behavior." She never answered my email, but the bus was not there an hour later.

It is necessary to make a distinction between the political leadership of Planned Parenthood and the direct services that they have provided to millions of people throughout many years and generations. The leadership appears to be heavily influenced in their strategic direction by the Democratic Party and as such reflects that historically defensive and compromising position. They are under continual right-wing attack as the "largest abortion provider in the country," and must be supported. Yet as the "largest abortion provider," they should take a far more proactive and uncompromising stance.

The closure of so many clinics, even with the availability of the pill, has been devastating for women's health. These are places for discussion, for counseling. An entire system of women's health care has been destroyed.

Many of the women who come to clinics are in crisis and have never engaged with the health care system. Many have never seen a gynecologist or had any primary care. Many also need referrals for multiple other stressors: some women are homeless, some are in violent relationships, some have immigration issues, and so forth. Their abortion is a gateway. Staff at clinics are usually prepared, and aware of where these women can access these ancillary services.

Many of the closures prior to *Dobbs* occurred in the middle of the country and in the South, where the majority of obstructionist legislative attempts and wins were. The costs for security alone are enormous. In 2011, for example, Texas had forty-six clinics; by September 2014, there were only a handful left. I watched this happen for years and, again, I did not see the deeper level of commitment required to fight it. I saw, instead, only a handful of individuals standing to sound the alarm. Sunsara Taylor was one of those people. The abortion rights emergency in the years leading up to *Dobbs* led to me working with Taylor on a bus tour of protests across the country.

As *Vice* reported at the time, we "gathered a crew of twenty-one fellow activists and embarked on a massive road trip—New York to Charlotte, North Carolina, by way of Fargo, Wichita, and Jackson, Mississippi. All for the purpose of demonstrating at last-remaining clinics, corrupt anti-abortion organizations, and state capitols. Their slogan: 'Abortion on Demand and Without Apology.' Their name, a provocative homage to another tremendous civil rights protest that toured the Deep South: the 'Abortion Rights Freedom Ride.'" From an activist's perspective, the reasons for the Freedom Ride were obvious: "Because there are all these attacks happening across the country," Sunsara told *Vice*, "we really wanted to connect up and actually lift people's heads to not just see these as local attacks but to see that there's a national war on women and we need more than fighting on a local basis, we need a national counteroffensive."

I had first met Sunsara in 1996 on the very first annual National Abortion Providers Appreciation Day. The day had been initiated a few years earlier when the mainstream medical establishment was distancing itself from abortion doctors and providers, who were being demonized, stigmatized, and hunted. Working at the time with Refuse and Resist, Taylor visited Choices, bringing a card and flowers.

Prior to the Abortion Rights Freedom Ride, the activists spent a full month in Texas doing speak-outs and civil disobediences. They went to Houston, Austin (where they were arrested), San Antonio, and down to the border region. They popularized the slogans "Abortion Providers Are He*Roes*," "Without Abortion Providers, There Is No Choice," and "Abortion On Demand and Without Apology!"

Despite the work, the backlash from other activists was immediate. The group Texans for Reproductive Justice issued a "United Statement in Opposition," stating that the organization "lacked transparency," and that "aside from the lack of transparency and questionable tactics, Stop Patriarchy is racist, Islamophobic, anti-sex worker, and anti-pornography." They accused the Freedom Ride of appropriating the language of slavery because the literature stated that forcing a woman to bear an unwanted child is "female enslavement." But our message was clear: Fetuses are not babies, and women are not incubators. Speaking to *The Cut*, Sunsara said:

> Providers are on the front lines, but the war on abortion is a war on women and it's going to have stakes that go way beyond any clinic. It's going to have effects on the social status of half of humanity when women are forced to have children against their will. Not only do they die from complications from pregnancy with much greater frequency, studies show, but women's lives are foreclosed on. They drop out of school, are driven into property, and trapped in abusive relationships. Forced pregnancy is a form of enslavement."[27]

Still, the activists were banned from pro-choice spaces because they didn't qualify as "pro-choice" by Texans for Reproductive Justice activists' definition. That is how far they went.

The Right to Choose: The Fundamental Question

Several months after *Dobbs*, the *New York Times* ran a piece in which they claimed that the fundamental question, when it comes to abortion, was when life begins. "In the months since the Supreme Court overturned *Roe v. Wade*, it has become unavoidable, as activists and politicians try to squeeze concrete answers from an eternal question of human existence."[28]

The article goes on:

> Lawmakers and judges from Arizona to South Carolina have been reviewing exactly which week of development during

---

27 Kat Stoeffel, "Q&A: The Pro-Choice Group Texas Feminists Hate," *The Cut*, July 29, 2014, https://www.thecut.com/2014/07/why-texas-feminists-hate-this-pro-choice-group.html.

28 Elizabeth Dias, "When Does Life Begin?" December 31, 2022, *New York Times*, https://www.nytimes.com/interactive/2022/12/31/us/human-life-begin.html.

pregnancy the procedure should be allowed. Some states draw the line at conception, or six weeks or 15 or around 40. Many others point to viability, the time when a fetus can survive outside the uterus. The implication is that after the determined time, the developing embryo or fetus is a human being with rights worth protecting.

Over the summer, when lawmakers in Indiana fought over passing a law banning most all abortions from conception, Republicans argued at length that a fertilized egg was a human life, at times citing their Christian principles—that "human life begins at conception" and "God our creator says you shall not murder." A Democrat pointed to another answer found in Title 35–31.5–2-160 of the Indiana code: "'Human being' means an individual who has been born and is alive." A disagreement over abortion policy became a fight over what it means to be human, the tension between conception and birth, church and state.

Indiana lawmakers were eventually able to resolve this tension over the "fundamental question" of when life begins by passing the near total abortion ban, which began in August 2023. But when life begins is *not* the fundamental question. The fundamental question is: Who is the chooser? What is the choice? The fundamental question is one of each woman's moral agency to make that determination. It is important to always remember: legal abortion *increases* the wantedness of each child. The children that a woman brings into this world should be planned and wanted—truly wanted. The question of when life begins is attractive to the opposition because it obviates the woman. Who are we talking about when we ask when life begins? We're talking about the fetus. We're not talking about the woman.

I go back to Nat Hentoff, who was a great liberal commentator, but profoundly anti-abortion. He compared fetuses to baby seals. "You know what they did with baby seals?" he would ask. A horrible image. Those beautiful little white faces with the big black eyes. "They are clubbing them to death." The difference is that a baby seal is not in utero. A fetus is part of a woman's body until it is not. Women have a fundamental, moral, human, civil right to decide when and whether they want to become mothers.

The most important thing is to have the psychological courage to articulate a fundamental shared truth: that legal safe abortion is necessary for the health and well-being of the mother and the family. In this current economic and social climate, the necessity is made obvious by the number of abortions. Is an abortion something we say every woman should have? No. Should we have systems and programs that support women who choose to have their children under the most difficult circumstances? Of course. I would be very pleased if we were living in a world where most women were deciding to go through with their pregnancies with knowledge, support, love, and safety. But it is crucial to ask why so many women aren't.

CHAPTER 6
RISING UP

Abortionomics

Many people fail to appreciate the profound impact economics has on one's decision to have an abortion. In the 1980s, it occurred to me to look into the data on the enormous volume that we were seeing at Choices. I was interested in understanding why all of these women were having abortions.

Working with a colleague at Adelphi University, I came up with a long questionnaire and distributed it to around two hundred patients. The results of this study were reported nationwide in articles with titles such as "Economy Prompts Abortion," "Tough Times Leading to More Abortions," "Rise in Abortions Due to Hard Economic Times," and "Reagan Policies Spurring Abortion Rates." One such paper, *The Kansas City Independence Examiner* reported that, "Fifty three percent of the women interviewed said financial reasons were the most important factor in deciding to have an abortion. In a similar study last year, only 28 percent cited economic reasons as their concern." (Reagan did have an answer to food insecurity in a time of major economic downturn: "Ketchup is a vegetable.")

What we found was that women's decisions to continue with a pregnancy were statistically significant in showing that the majority of women made the decision to have an abortion because of economic reasons. The age groups fell evenly between 18 and 39, incomes ranged from $11,000 to $20,000 yearly, 65 percent worked; 35 percent were the sole support of their families; 28 percent were married. Many had never believed in abortion; many saw it as killing. However, faced with the reality of economic survival, 35 percent said they had to change their value system. And so, these women who have suffered most, who have been forced into a corner by financial considerations, who have made their decisions in pain, are accosted and frightened and verbally abused by those who would impose their own wills on everyone else.

This only reinforced what I was hearing and seeing every day with our patients. It was astonishing to me that in the 2022 midterm elections, these two issues were always cast as separate poles. Should the Democratic party stress economics or abortion? They are joined at the hip—and not only through my own research. Can we not walk and chew gum at the same time?

The general disrespect of women will lead the Antis to claim, "It's not that they can't afford to raise another child; it's that they want to have another car or another TV." They attack women on the fundamental American canon and creed—consumerism. This consumer patriotism was articulated by President George W. Bush on the evening of the 9/11 attacks when he told the public that the "American economy was still open for business." He also told people to "get down to Disney World in Florida." So, now having an abortion for economic reasons is a crime against consumer patriotism.

Of course, the economic reasons that women stated for having an abortion are most often related to survival: food, clothing, shelter, other children. For a country that has almost no social support for mothers or families, thinking that women will abort to buy another TV or to "look good in their bathing suits" is beyond comment. There are other reasons—reasons that you and I may not agree with—but that is the meaning of the phrase "trust women," which George Tiller popularized. Not the state, not the Supreme Court, and not some legislators. Trust women to know what is best for them and their families.

There is a myriad of other reasons that women want or need to have an abortion. I remember a patient who came to Choices with her husband. She was eighteen weeks pregnant according to a previous sonogram. When the counselor asked why she wanted an abortion, she said it was because the fetus was female, and she did not want to have another female child. The counselor came to me, conflicted, and asked me to intervene. I sat with the woman and listened to her as she explained that it was boys that were most desired in her country and culture. I reminded her that she was now living in the United States, but it soon became clear to me that her mind and heart were still in Pakistan.

I realized in that powerful moment that I would never make the same decision for that reason. The feminist in me thought, *How could someone terminate this fetus just because it is female like me?* Yet the pro-choice part thought, *It is her choice.* You have to separate the *chooser* from the *choice.* You will not always agree with the chooser, nor respect the choice, but you must trust that she knows what is best.

My goal in anything I do publicly is to inject some truth into the dialogue, to try to bring the reality of all my experience, the reality of women's lives, and all that I have seen over the last half-century. It is not about the definition of when life begins. It is not about the politics of this referendum or the next one, this state or that state. It is about women and individual women's lives. As Dr. George Tiller would say, "Abortion is not a cerebral or a reproductive issue. Abortion is a matter of the heart: for until one understands the heart of a woman, nothing about abortion makes any sense at all."

In 2012, I presented a much-expanded Abortionomics study on the impact of recession on abortion—done in conjunction with Akeso Consulting and this time with 500 patients—at the National Press Club. *Washington Post* columnist Dana Milbank was in the audience that day and in response to my presentation, he wrote an attack column[29] against me claiming my concerns over abortion were totally hyperbolic.

"Abortion rates have exploded since the economic collapse, [Hoffman] warned, as nearly three-quarters of women ending their pregnancies say they simply can't afford to have a baby. Hoffman expanded on that trend to forecast a 'dim future' for women if

---

29 Dana Milbank, "Roe v. Wade's Greedy Offspring," *Washington Post,* January 17, 2012, https://www.washingtonpost.com/opinions/roe-v-wade-and-the-dishonest-industry-it-spawned/2012/01/17/gIQAaf5T6P_story.html.

a Republican wins the White House: a world of abortion 'slave states' and 'underground railroads' and 'pre-*Roe* reality.'"

And yet here we are.

"If the 'choice' rally participants really wanted to preserve legal abortion," he went on, "they'd be wise to drop the sky-is-falling warnings about *Roe* and to acknowledge that the other side, and most Americans, have legitimate concerns. Not every compromise means a slippery slope to the back alley.

"But this is no time for reason; this is time for collecting donations. At the Press Club, abortion provider Hoffman gave a full-throated defense of her own abortion ('I had committed myself to my work' and didn't want to be 'diverted'), coupled with dire warnings about the future of legal abortion ('relentless attacks … will be impossible'). Hoffman likened her defense of the procedure to Martin Luther's 95 Theses. 'Abortion is a life-affirming act,' she said, and 'abortion is often the most moral choice.' Abortion as a 'most moral" and 'life-affirming' choice? It's beginning to feel a lot like *Roe* week in Washington. (Donate now.)"

There were multiple letters of support published after the column ran. As journalist and author Irin Carmon wrote in *Slate*:

To say this smacks of the airy privilege of someone who isn't directly affected by the situation is an understatement. . . . That's not just because Milbank is a man; it's also because he probably doesn't know anyone who can't afford an abortion, can't access one, or was forced through intentionally odious obstacles before getting one. (And if somehow he does, he needs an empathy check.) The same goes for his mockery of Hoffman's position that abortion can be a moral or "life-affirming" choice, in which he adopts a smug posture toward a woman who actually had an abortion and works daily with other women who have too. Somehow, he knows better.

So, what does it mean when the majority of women who have abortions cite economic circumstances as the reason? We live in a country where economic growth and consumerism are viewed both as the engine driving the system and the goal—the means and the end. And maternal deaths have doubled since 1999, with the most among Black women. The United States is the richest, most scientifically advanced nation in the world—in the history of the world—and look at where we are in terms of the care we give to mothers. Look at the statistics for Black women and minority women. From 1990 to 2015, the average mortality rate in the US increased from 12 to 14 deaths per 100,000 live births. That number puts the United States at the 46th place in the world. According to the CDC[30]:

> Overall pregnancy-related mortality in the United States occurs at an average rate of 17.2 deaths per 100,000 live births. Leading causes of death include cardiovascular conditions, hemorrhage, and infection. However, in the Netherlands, Norway, and New Zealand, that rate drops to 3 or fewer women per 100,000.
>
> When it comes to care providers, the United States and Canada "have the lowest overall supply of midwives and obstetrician-gynecologists (OB-GYNs)—12 and 15 providers per 1000 live births, respectively," whereas all other countries have a supply that is between 2 and 6 times greater. Midwives differ from OB-GYNs in that they help manage a normal pregnancy, assist with childbirth, and provide care during the postpartum period. In contrast, OB-GYNs are physicians trained to identify issues and intervene should abnormal conditions arise. OB-GYNs typically only provide care in hospital-based settings. The role of midwives has been found to be comparable or preferable to physician-led care in terms of mother and baby outcomes and more efficient use of health care resources.

From the structure and economics of the health care system itself, to the institutional racism and lack of access for millions, to the abysmal rating of our maternal mortality and morbidity statics

---

30 Sherry L. Murphy, Kenneth D. Kochanek, Jiaquan Xu, and Elizabeth Arias, "Mortality in the United States, 2020," CDC, NCHS Data Brief No. 427 (December 2021), https://www.cdc.gov/nchs/products/databriefs/db427.htm#section_5.

in comparison to the rest of the developed world—the reality and the overriding message is that women and children just don't matter.

Now, we have a perfect storm of rising inflation, lack of any kind of true support for mothers and children, and the draconian stripping of women's fundamental right to choose. As inflation is really hitting people, families have to be even more careful about how they will afford to care for a child. Everything is becoming more expensive, and that includes raising children.

Acta Non Verba

At the bottom of my correspondence, I often use the phrase *acta non verba*: action, not words. There are many defenses against reality. Over time those defenses become walls, walls that trap empathy, imagination, and compassion. We must always look at the reality and we must act. For over fifty years, I have seen women with no masks. They are in crisis. They are moving through a precarious life event. They do not have the luxury of living in a narrated, formulaic space, and so neither should I.

What is lacking is a sense of empathy—radical empathy. And a lack of imagination that has been invaded by incessant images from popular culture. When I was studying to become a pianist, I played and loved the music of Chopin. There was a myth that only Polish people could play Chopin because it was in their blood, that the specific structure and tempo of Chopin's mazurkas were beyond anyone who did not share Chopin's ethnicity. I never understood that, and never believed it. I could empathize with Chopin just as I could empathize with Bach, even though I'm not German. Many people cannot or will not picture themselves in the position of a woman for whom it is necessary to have an abortion. It is so much easier to say, "Well, I would never be in that position." But again, that is not the reality of the world we live in. So many patients over the years have said to me, "I really have an issue with abortion. I'm not like those other women out there in the waiting room. I'm different. Life didn't catch me. Something else happened." Life catches all of us, and we must judge ourselves not by being caught, but by the ways in which we react to those myriad circumstances out of our control.

A Silent Constituency: Coming Out of the Abortion Closet

Abortion is the bloody part of feminism. It is the theory in practice. Women who are in what can be the loneliest of times of their lives (facing an unwanted pregnancy) are in reality not alone. For each woman who has a legal abortion, there are thousands like her who, before 1973, submitted to the horrors of illegal abortion and millions upon millions who contemplate the possibility of an abortion when periods are late or missed. Now, the personal must once again become the political. No longer is there the luxury of putting one's pain away, of silently and personally integrating. The right has made abortion an all-too-public act. Privacy, the constitutional issue that legalization was based on, is now invalidated. Time for more courage—more commitment. Time to testify. Once again, women must be able to say strongly, "Yes, I, too, have had an abortion. By making my choice and acting on that choice with my mind and body, I have added my political voice." We need no further example of what happens when we do not heed the words of Edmund Burke, the father of conservatism: "Let not any one pacify his conscience by the delusion that he can do no harm if he takes no part, and forms no opinion. Bad men need nothing more to compass their ends, than that good men should look on and do nothing."

There are, of course, those for whom the testimony won't matter. All the horror stories, all the families and lives torn apart will always be in soft focus. "A baby is a gift from God," they will say. "You have to find a way to welcome it, even though it might ruin your life and your family." Once at a rally, an anti-abortion woman came up to me to tell me that she had had an abortion and regretted it ever since. If every woman who has an abortion regrets their decision, it's still not an argument against the choice to have an abortion. *Women have the right to make the wrong choice.* People run away from the realities of life. They don't want to have regrets. They don't want to have conflicts. They want everybody to validate their fears and their triggers and their feelings. They want to be safe, but again there are no safe spaces for women and girls. This is not life—at least not life as I've seen it and lived it. This is, rather, preparing people to be children for their entire lives. What does a child need? Direction. Who gives direction? The parent. Who is the parent in this case? It must be the woman who parents herself—she must become responsible for her decision—not the state. As we stated in one of the earliest chants: "Not the Church. Not the State—WOMEN MUST DECIDE THEIR FATE."

In a sense abortion is as American as apple pie. Women must come out of their abortion closets and into the public's gaze. The first step must be internal—recognizing that you made that choice; that your ability to have made that choice in the last half century was due to the work and struggle of so many women before you; that your continued existence in the life that you are now leading is the result of your ability to have made the choice. The second part is up to you and your comfort level—perhaps telling friends and family, volunteering, donating. But you must ultimately move into the political—into the streets—because nothing but a mass uprising of individuals will make a difference in obstructing this march toward the fascist control of women's lives and bodies.

The Antis, Post-*Dobbs*

Regardless of the challenge, the Antis will continue to be pro-active and resourceful. They will appeal to environmental issues, to health concerns, to criminalization of the abortion pill, working to extend rights to fetuses from conception that equal and will at times trump the woman's. They will use every possible avenue to stop women from attempting to control their own reproduction. This is why it is as important as ever to listen to them, to take them at their word, believe what they say, and find ways to stop them.

One anti-abortion group sent a "petition asking the Food and Drug Administration to require any doctor who prescribes the pills to be responsible for disposing of the fetal tissue—which anti-abortion advocates want to be bagged and treated as medical waste rather than flushed down the toilet and into the wastewater," according to Politico.[31] In the same article, Susan Wood, the former FDA assistant commissioner for women's health and a professor of health policy at George Washington University, points out that "It seems like they're laying the groundwork for considering contraception itself as medical waste."

House Majority Leader Steve Scalise (R-LA) was quoted saying that "*Dobbs* was only the first phase of this battle." Two measures were passed by House Republicans after taking power. One of the bills increases the protections for an infant born after an attempted abortion. (The other, a resolution, condemns violence against facilities, groups, and churches opposed to abortions.) There have been actual "wrongful birth" cases.

Fetal personhood is also another ripe area for legislation and litigation. Supporters of fetal personhood want to confer legal rights from the moment of conception. This goes far beyond bans, "compromises at fifteen weeks," etc. But there is good news here: In Georgia, a fetus now can qualify for tax credits, child support, and is included in the population counts and redistricting.

There was a case of a woman driving in the HOV lane in New York (High Occupancy Vehicle; 2 people or more) who, when pulled over by a police officer for not having anyone else in the car, said she was pregnant, and the fetus was the second person with her. That seems like a perfectly fine defense, but would, out of necessity, require all traffic cops to be trained as sonographers.

A little imaginative thinking will take you to other areas in which a fetus could actually be given rights—immigration public funds come to mind. A case could be made for any pregnant migrant to be denied immigration status because they have a second

31 Alice Miranda Ollstein, "The Next Abortion Fight Could Be Over Wastewater Regulation," *Politico*, November 23, 2022, https://www.politico.com/news/2022/11/23/abortion-pills-opponents-environmental-laws-00070603.

person—or we might develop laws that would accept the mother but not the "unborn child" to reduce immigration—and fetuses could possibly gain legal "standing" for a class action suit on government funding for their care and or other financial benefits.

The Pill

Perhaps the area of greatest focus for the Antis will be on the abortion pill—mifepristone. Indeed, this battle has already begun.

Mifepristone was developed in the 1980s and approved in the United States in 2000. As part of the executive branch of the National Abortion Federation (NAF), I and others were given our own presentation by Danco Laboratories regarding the pill coming to the US before it was even approved by the FDA. The discussion centered not only the medical aspects of how easy and available the pill could be for women, but also how this would be the "knight on the white horse," saving the movement from all the anti-abortion attacks at clinics. Now that women would have the pill, the thinking went, they wouldn't need clinics, they wouldn't have to endure harassment by protesters, clinics wouldn't be bombed, and doctors wouldn't be killed. An abortion could, finally and truly, be between a patient and her doctor. An abortion would be a private act, just as *Roe v. Wade* envisioned it, between a woman and her doctor in the first trimester. At the time, this felt like it would throw a massive wrench into the opposition's plans.

When it came out in France, the health minister called it "the moral property of women." I thought that was beautiful. (I would have liked to see an international law declaring that women's bodies and women's choices about when and whether to be mothers is also the moral property of women. A girl can dream.) I thought the pill would be a great leap forward, particularly for women who did not have clinics geographically readily available to them.

However, when someone presents a utopian solution to a complex problem, I maintain my skepticism. I was skeptical of the pill because I could see how it would lead people to, once again, minimize the opposition. I remember thinking to myself that the Antis would find a way to discover exactly which doctors and pharmacies were prescribing and providing the pills and do whatever they could to obstruct distribution. Unfortunately, I was very prescient, witnessing the plethora of current legislative attempts to go after the pill.

Anything that would move these issues forward scientifically and medically is a positive. Anything that can expand access and reduce stress and the potential for complications is progress. However, this does not obviate the other issues having to do with taking the pill in general and ensuring that there is enough education. Women must know what to do or who to call should complications arise, or for counseling.

My concerns are the women who are who involved in intimate, violent relationships and the women in prison. How can they access an abortion? How can they get the support they need if the only thing you can do is get a pill, and then you are with someone who watches your every move? There are gestational limitations to consider as well. The FDA only approved the pill up to ten weeks (though many providers use the pill up to twelve or thirteen weeks). What worried me in the beginning was the thinking that the pill would make a fundamental difference in women being able to access abortion without stress, harassment, or fear. All of these issues were the ones that I initially debated with the activists who were attacking RiseUp because we did not see the pill as this knight on a white horse. Everything that is currently going on proves that these concerns were valid.

At first, the pill was not used frequently. It was presented as an option but because most women had access to clinics that specialized in surgical procedures, most of them chose the surgical procedure. It is a ten-minute procedure for a first trimester abortion, with a recovery time of up to two hours, as opposed to having to take two sets of pills, deliver the fetus in a safe space—usually a toilet—and come back for a follow-up. With a surgical procedure, it is a one-day event and when you go home, you are no longer pregnant.

The majority of abortions were surgical until the states began to obstruct access by putting restrictions on clinics. As more clinics closed, the pill became more attractive, especially with the rise in popularity of telemedicine during the Covid-19 pandemic. During the pandemic, all surgical services in outpatient surgery centers were paused indefinitely, except for "essential procedures." In New York and other states there was a move to define abortion as non-essential. We were able to argue strongly enough on this point, and Choices never closed during the entire pandemic. Within 100 days of the *Dobbs* decision, over sixty clinics had closed across the United States. With the loss of so many clinics, the popularity of the pill has increased considerably. By 2023, nearly 51 percent of women who are choosing to terminate a pregnancy in the first trimester use the pill.

The opposition has already gone after distributors and consumers alike. With consumers—patients—they have already been successful by building outposts in their heads—stigma, stigma, stigma. Women are "killing babies." Doctors are murderers. This transcends the actual method of abortion. It doesn't matter if it is a pill or a surgical procedure, as long as women believe these narratives—and so many do—they have incredible hurdles to overcome. With distributors, they will continue to protest, harass, and boycott. They will use whatever laws they can to disrupt the distribution. They may not have the means to go after the drug companies, which can afford lengthy litigation, but they have already begun to go after the mom-and-pop pharmacies, the small-town doctors writing the prescriptions, and the large national chains like CVS and Walgreens. And they can flood social media with disinformation.

In November 2022, a group of anti-abortion activists filed a lawsuit against the FDA, intentionally seeking out a Trump-appointed conservative judge in Texas. The suit, according to *Gothamist*, "asserts that the FDA did not adequately assess the safety of the drug when it was first approved in September 2000. The plaintiffs also challenged other regulations around abortion medication, arguing that the federal government has put people at increased risk by making it easier to obtain over the years."[32] Twenty-two state attorneys general, siding with the Antis, "argued that the ability to send mifepristone by mail infringes upon the ability of each state to establish its own abortion regulations." If the judge were to block access to the pill, the ruling would affect women even in states where abortion is legal. As I told *Gothamist*: "It's not only dystopian, it's just unbelievable that they're deciding which medications we can take. I do not consider any state in this country safe."

Access is critical. The opposition is already protesting in front of pharmacies. The idea of a federal approval that would make the pill readily available in all fifty states is a very good one. The possibility of it coming into being is another question. At this point in time, abortion has not only been politicized and weaponized, but medicalized. There was a time that abortion was done either by some mixture of herbs and chemicals, or "surgical abortions" that were in the hands of women who trained themselves as Madame Restelle did (using whale bone).[33] By the late 1800s, with the rise of Comstock and the moral panic he brought, men realized that they could become doctors relatively easily and began to define and take over the entire obstetrical and abortion field.[34] Now, one needs a clinic or a hospital, an OR, a medical doctor; there are regulations, licenses, procedures.

The Antis understand this, and they have been effective at finding multiple ways to combat the supply side of the equation. But from time immemorial, women have had the knowledge and the

---

32 Caroline Lewis, "How Abortion Pill Access in New York is Threatened by a Texas Court," *Gothamist*, February 21, 2023, https://gothamist.com/news/abortion-medication-mifepristone-ny-threatened-texas-court-what-case-could-mean-for-your-access.

33 For a fascinating look at the life of the infamous nineteenth-century "Abortionist of Fifth Avenue," see Jennifer Wright's *Madame Restell: The Life, Death, and Resurrection of Old New York's Most Fabulous, Fearless, and Infamous Abortionist.*

34 The Comstock Act of 1873, which made it illegal to send "obscene, lewd or lascivious," "immoral," or "indecent" publications through the mail, including writings pertaining to contraception and abortion, is making a comeback among the Antis. Supreme Court Justice Samuel Alito referenced the act in the *Dobbs* decision. In an attempt to ban the abortion pill, a Trump-appointed judge actually cited the Comstock Act as recently as April 2023.

instinct to terminate a pregnancy when they know, in that moment, that they cannot bring another life into the world. Women have always understood this.

Resisting the Rapid Normalization of *Dobbs*

The normalization of *Dobbs* is perhaps the greatest challenge for the pro-choice movement. The Antis have effectively changed the theater of war. Now, the battles are raging in many states. No one is taking seriously the idea of a federally protected right to abortion. Biden has been quoted as saying there is absolutely nothing he can do at the executive level (even though Biden and Vice President Harris called for the reinstatement of *Roe* by Congress). So, we have to make the best of it. We should pin our hopes on the individual states in terms of a political process and the pill.

Struggling to gain a right is often a long and arduous process. The fight to gain the right to vote had many martyrs—as did the civil rights struggle. Most of these were activists consciously willing to risk their lives for the cause. The initial struggle for legal abortion, which resulted in *Roe*, had *thousands* of martyrs—and not by choice. These were the women who risked and often lost their lives on dirty kitchen tables or attempting to self-abort. They had no voice—*Roe* gave them that voice. We have lost that now—and though we may have leaders and spokespersons who articulate this reality . . . everyone who has been touched by this issue must find their voice.

Once you lose a right, it is very difficult to reclaim it. The question, of course, is how to maintain it. You have to do everything you can do. The rule of law can crumble. We acknowledge that we weren't proactive enough, and we didn't believe it could happen. We did not take the opposition at their word. We didn't listen to them before, but we better listen to them now: they're saying that their end game is a total national ban on abortion. Many opportunities to codify abortion rights nationally have arisen. There was a vote on it as recently as the summer of 2021. Politicians just did not list it as a priority, and the nonprofits and the pro-choice organizations were not pushing hard enough to make codifying *Roe* issue number one—when they should have. It was a matter of complacency, of compromise, and of playing politics—of moving in lockstep with the party. And it cost women dearly.

With RiseUp, I was determined to tell the truth: that abortion must be legal and accessible across the country. Otherwise, there are free states and slave states for women, regardless of what Dana Milbank may think. I am, of course, still waiting for his apology. Since *Dobbs*, the strategy and tactics have come down from the White House and Planned Parenthood. All the national pro-choice organizations and nonprofit organizations have focused their efforts on raising money for women from states that have banned abortion, in order to provide them with services in states where abortion was still legal. That is a necessary and noble cause. But it is also in some sense a surrender. In actuality, we are funding our own oppression! No money is going into the fight, no one is funding the activism, the rallies, the literature. Nothing is being done to *raise hell*. The Democratic Party's strategy is not to harness the rage, but to ensure women can travel.

RiseUp's agenda was political. Our way was the way of resistance. By 2022, it had been twenty years since I was last on a soapbox. I had not done any public-facing radical action on the street for many years—no one had. In the last two decades, I was inundated with Choices; adopted a three-and-a-half-year-old girl from from Siberia; lost my husband, mother, and closest friend; and also wrote and published my memoir *Intimate Wars*, which required a great deal of attention. Until *Dobbs*, I had not been out in public in the same way in quite some time.

After *Dobbs*, I was looking around at what was happening. What I found was frightening: *nothing was happening*. Publicly or in the streets. It was so quiet. There was no question what I had to do. Someone had to do something—anything—even if it was standing in front of the Supreme Court and speaking out. It was obvious, too, that the opposition was aware of how disorganized our side was. I remember after the Freedom Ride to Texas, one of the senators or congressmen said it was an "open season" on abortion rights. The Antis have eyes everywhere. When they expand on existing restrictions or create new ones, and there is no great outcry, they know they can go a little further. Historically, Texas has been the leader in passing restrictive requirements and laws on abortion. When their actions didn't wake people up, that was it. They just kept pushing.

Texas has a history of anti-abortion legislation going back to 1999, when they required parental notification for minors seeking abortions; in 2013, when they required doctors providing abortions to have limits to their admitting privileges on medical abortions and prohibiting abortion after twenty weeks; or in 2022, when the trigger law went into effect. (According to a recent study from the researchers from the Johns Hopkins Bloomberg School of Public Health found that 9,800 additional babies were born in Texas in a nine-month period after the State banned abortions after six weeks.[35])

After the *Dobbs* hearing in late December 2021, Sunsara Taylor, with whom I'd worked on the Texas action, contacted me about getting together to do something. Sunsara was introduced to me by Mary Lou Greenberg, with whom I worked with for over thirty years. Mary Lou came into my life when I was forming the New York Pro-Choice Coalition in the 1990s, when we needed an organized opposition and controlled response because Operation Rescue, led by Randall Terry, was invading and closing clinics.

When Mary Lou first came to see me, she wanted to know about the coalition, and said to me, "You know, I'm a communist."

"So what?" I said. "You believe that women must have this right, and you will fight for it. I want you to come and join us."

As they say, perfectionism is the enemy of excellence. I believe that polemics limit progress and progressive politics. In my mind, you must make as broad a coalition as possible. My concern is not what each faction is hoping to get out of it. The fact that one group

---

35 Bell S. O., Stuart E. A., Gemmill A., "Texas' 2021 Ban on Abortion in Early Pregnancy and Changes in Live Births." *JAMA*. https://pubmed.ncbi.nlm.nih.gov /37382968/.

may view your issue as a stepping stone to another, or view the issue in a different light, is not the issue. My concern is that we are pushing the agenda of ensuring women have the right to safe abortions without being harassed and without doctors being murdered. That has been and always will be my only concern.

My political inclusivity has led me to very interesting places and to work with individuals—individuals, like Sunsara Taylor, with end goals very different from my own. Sunsara started out as a young activist, and through Mary Lou became involved with Bob Avakian, chairman of the Revolutionary Communist Party (RCP).

We all knew *Dobbs* would come in June. Lori Sokol (editor of *Women's E-News* and longtime feminist) was also responding to the public silence and in her frustration had joined with Sunsara to reach out to me. They wanted my participation to organize a response to wake people up to what was happening. This was good news to me. The three of us got on a Zoom to discuss the statement Sunsara had drafted, which a number well-known activists such as Cornel West, Gloria Steinem, Phyllis Chesler, and V (formerly known as Eve Ensler) signed.

WE REFUSE TO LET THE U.S. SUPREME COURT DENY WOMEN'S HUMANITY AND DECIMATE THEIR RIGHTS!

WE CALL ON EVERYONE TO JOIN US IN FIGHTING FOR:

ABORTION ON DEMAND AND WITHOUT APOLOGY!

Now is the time for *everyone* who believes that women and girls are *full human beings*—not incubators—to act to *prevent a great horror.*

The Supreme Court stands poised to gut and very possibly overturn the landmark 1973 *Roe v. Wade* decision that established the right of women to abortion. A decision is expected by late spring. This comes on top of hundreds of restrictions that effectively deny this essential right to huge numbers of women already. This could trigger more than 20 states to immediately ban or severely restrict abortion.

The attack on abortion rights is part of a patriarchal Christian fascist program that takes aim at contraception as well as LGBTQ rights. Denying the right to abortion hits poor women, and especially Black and other women of color, with vicious consequence—tightening the chains of *both* white supremacy *and* the subjugation of women.

Denying the right to abortion forces women to bear children against their will. This does grotesque physical, emotional, societal, and psychic violence to women by reducing them to baby-making machines! Compelling women to carry unwanted and/or dangerous pregnancies hijacks their bodies, their safety, their lives, their sexual autonomy, their aspirations and accomplishments, and their life-long relations in the service of patriarchal domination.

Forced motherhood is female enslavement. **When women are not free, no one is free.**

Yet all too many pro-choice leaders and Democratic Party politicians preach a "realism" of accepting the Court's gutting of abortion rights. They tell us to dig in for the "long-haul" of the electoral process or to focus on helping women induce their own abortions. Whatever their intent, this amounts to *capitulating in advance* to the enslavement of women and an overall nightmare for humanity.

The violent subjugation of half of society must not be accommodated, excused, downplayed, or surrendered to. IT MUST BE STOPPED!

RISING UP

If we leave this to Congress, the Courts, and State Legislatures and do not fill the streets with people determined to stop this, then there is virtually no hope for stopping this assault. *But if we, in our multitudes, stand up in uncompromising defiance then there is a possibility—not a certainty, but a real possibility—that we could beat back this assault and begin to change the whole political dynamic in this country.*

***Our only way forward and* our *best way forward* is to *resist.* To step outside the confines of "official" politics and fill the streets with our fury.** Growing in numbers, in cities and small towns, uniting all who can be united and coming back stronger in continuing, sustained, nonviolent mass protest. Shaking all of society from the streets to the arts and sciences with our determination. Drawing inspiration from the mighty outpourings of women and others around the world against patriarchal degradation. Changing the whole political atmosphere throughout society and what women-haters—from the Supreme Court to the State Houses to the streets—feel they can get away with. **Rising up with courage and conviction to *defeat* this assault while bringing closer a future where women and all people are free.**

On January 22, the anniversary of *Roe v. Wade*, we begin. In the face of triumphalist patriarchal Marches for "Life," we will announce to the world that a force is gathering to defeat this through massive, relentless, nonviolent action of people of all genders. Gather in DC at NOON at the Supreme Court. Other places TBA.

On March 8, International Women's Day, we come back with creativity and growing numbers in small towns and the big cities, filling the streets with serious determination and rebellious joy. We will puncture the stifling atmosphere of capitulation to a great injustice and compel all to take notice, inspiring more people to join us. We start organizing *now.*

From there, we rally more people and fury and moral clarity . . . aiming to *bring society to a halt* and force our demand—that women *not be slammed backwards*—to be reckoned with and *acted upon* by every institution in society.

Sign this statement. Spread it everywhere. Donate generously. **Use this statement to organize growing networks** across this country of people from different backgrounds and genders, creeds and political outlooks, united in our unwavering refusal to see women enslaved.

If you care about the half of humanity that is born female . . . **if you remember the dark days of back-alley deaths and foreclosed lives . . . if you are among the 1 in 4 women whose hopes and dreams—or even survival—has hinged on access to abortion** . . . **if you refuse to inherit, or pass on, a world that is hurtling backwards . . .**

NOW is the time to hold nothing back. *NOW* is the time to rouse thousands and soon millions in struggle so that we can look every woman and girl in the eye with the promise in word and deed that they will have a future as *full human beings*. *NOW* is the time to stand up, together, as if our lives depend upon it—for, in fact, they do.

Once this was published, we decided to go to the Supreme Court on January 22, the anniversary of *Roe v. Wade*. That became our first event we did as officially RiseUp. We liked the idea of a "rising"—of people waking up and rising up, all of us, for abortion rights.

There's a romance in speaking at rallies. There's a romance in standing up for the truth. This is where all the warrior fantasies come in—me, standing alone to protect the truth. I feel alive when I am giving speeches. It was apparent from the first time I did it that this was my life's purpose. I had spent so much time fantasizing about Elizabeth, Joan, all these visionary, great, powerful women, and then I could finally feel the reality of it.

When I went to the Supreme Court, I was nervous. I hadn't given a soapbox speech in a long time. I remember the train ride to Washington with Lori. It was her first time giving a public speech, so she was going over it and over it, writing, editing, and rehearsing. Lori's voice was important in that moment because she focused on what *Dobbs* would mean for the LGBTQ+ community, how the Supreme Court's decision would spread into anti-gay and -trans legislation—which it did with a vengeance. She was nervous, too, and excited, as was I. The minute I got up there, it felt like home.

We woke people up to the fact that this fundamental right was being stripped away. Our actions—and the reactions to our actions—moved the conversation forward at the White House. Biden became more focused and assertive in his claims about fighting the decision. I was invited to be on a Zoom meeting at the White House to learn about the strategy and how they were moving toward a more comprehensive answer to what happened with *Roe*. There was a definite *slight* shift in their spin.

We did so many creative things, and we gave people a place to positively channel their anger and hopelessness. Anger can so easily turn on itself and become depression and despair. This only creates passivity. The anger, again, must be channeled into righteous rage. After the RiseUp rallies, so many women came up to me and told me it was the first time they had come out. They never thought they would have to. That we were able to direct those feelings externally was remarkable.

I was not surprised by the level of rage, because I see it every day. But I was delighted that anger is there because women are realizing that they now are second-class citizens in this country. It just needs an outlet; it needs articulating. What surprised and moved me was an older woman coming up to me at the first or second rally while a young woman, maybe fifteen years old, was giving a speech with tears in her eyes. The older woman said, "I'm so sorry we couldn't keep this right for you." There was this tremendous sense of guilt and responsibility. Now mothers will have to have a conversation with their daughters about how to navigate this life without choice.

With RiseUp, there was a true rising. We inspired thousands and thousands of people across the country and throughout the world to get involved. We had ten people on January 22, 2022, and over the following months thousands of young people came out in support of our cause. Many of them became political for the first time. They found their voices. They got on stage and spoke. There is, if you can tap into it, a youthful rage against this kind of authority, especially with the burgeoning understanding of how much it will impact their lives. They articulated their passion to a huge number of people. This was an extraordinary achievement for each of the individuals and for RiseUp itself.

This work is a calling in every sense of the word. And 2022 was one of the most extraordinary years of my life. It was one of those years in which everything became political. There is nothing comparable to the feeling of expressing your total self—every part of you in service to a greater cause. But you have to be ready for the blowback.

Working with people is not always easy. It can be complicated, especially when you are coming from different ideological corners. We're creatures that need community. We need people. We need socialization. We need to feel not only that our lives have meaning to ourselves, but that that meaning can be shared.

If I were to choose the two most important qualities necessary for building or working in coalitions, they would be the ability not to personalize every interaction and the ability to situationally put aside ego needs. This is not easy, especially for women who need to be liked, to be accepted.

Women haven't had the history of dealing politically, publicly, for as long as men, and because there has been so little public space for deserved recognition, these two qualities are challenging. Add to that the exquisite awareness that the "woke" culture has grafted onto speech, resulting in the formation of like-minded groups and groupthink. Nobody likes to be attacked, and most people like to be agreed with. (I'm unusual. I like to debate.)

Everyone, it seems, can be triggered. In reality, life triggers us. We should learn and teach others how to lean into those triggers. The call for safe spaces provided by institutions or government is a utopian fantasy. By "leaning in," I mean practicing courage, learning resilience, and being ready for what life throws at you. I agree with Hamlet that "readiness is all."

With Sunsara, we would talk and debate over ideological disagreements more than strategic ones, and it was often very productive. We also brought those discussions to the public through Sunsara's TV program *The RNL—Revolution, Nothing Less!* We wanted to be role models for how two political people could respectfully disagree on fundamental principles. But eventually I would hit a wall, and that wall was her absolute belief that our system was broken and that in order to get true social justice and equality, we had to start over—a (new) communist revolution. Having studied the history of the French and Communist Revolutions, this was not a place I wanted to work toward or live in.

Which Side Are You On?

The day after the *Dobbs* decision, a group of leftist grassroots feminist activists started to attack RiseUp. They did not want to work with the "communists" or Sunsara Taylor. They made blatantly false allegations of financial wrongdoing in a "Statement Against RiseUp4AbortionRights" written and published by NYC for Abortion Rights and reprinted here in full.

> We, a coalition of grassroots pro-abortion organizers, publicly denounce RiseUp for Abortion Rights.
>
> Our movement needs to be strong and united. Most repro groups have turned their backs on RiseUp privately since their inception. It is vital for all repro groups to now unite in discrediting RiseUp publicly.
>
> Below is a non-exhaustive list of our concerns about RiseUp,

and why we strongly urge pro-abortion activists to join us in rejecting its leadership and demanding the group step back from pro-abortion spaces:

RiseUp is a cult and pyramid scheme.

RiseUp is an offshoot of the RevCom (Revolutionary Communist Party) group. Over the past few decades, RevCom has emerged as a personality cult revolving around its white male leader Bob Avakian. While RevCom fervently denies accusations of it being a cult, RevCom's own website claims the only effective way to achieve social change is to follow Avakian's leadership and teachings. Similar to its parent group RevCom, RiseUp's only goal appears to be gaining more followers in order to raise more and more money. Both essentially function as pyramid schemes that prey on social movements.

RiseUp diverts money from social and racial justice movements.

RevCom and its fronts—RiseUp and Refuse Fascism—are notorious for raising tens of thousands of dollars and using those funds to pay RevCom leadership, and to purchase marketing materials (to raise even more money). Refuse Fascism exploits civil unrest to recruit followers (as it did during the 2014 and 2020 uprisings), and RiseUp is now repeating the same scheme. The RiseUp website, for instance, features urgent prompts to donate with no information about where this money goes. What we do know is that this money never goes to abortion funds (which they argue are not a strategy to defend abortion access), providers, practical support groups, or anyone actually working to increase abortion access.

RiseUp stigmatizes abortion and perpetuates harmful myths.

RiseUp is currently focused on its "Save Roe" campaign, which involves the wearing of white pants painted with fake blood, die-ins, and coat-hanger imagery. These theatrical tactics further the extremely harmful idea that abortion is a violent procedure and safe self-managed abortion is not possible. In fact, RiseUp has not once raised awareness about medication abortion as a post-Roe tool, and its only aim is "saving Roe," despite this never having been enough historically.

RiseUp perpetuates anti-Blackness and does not center intersectionality.

RiseUp's leader, Sunsara Taylor, has been a controversial figure in pro-abortion spaces. She and her followers are known for swooping into town and leeching off of existing BIPOC-led grassroots efforts across the country. Additionally, RiseUp frequently likens abortion bans to "female enslavement," which is profoundly disrespectful to Black, Indigenous, and POC comrades.

RiseUp has a homophobic past, and remains transphobic.

RiseUp leadership frequently others trans and non-binary folks and excludes them from its speeches, writing, and conversations. In responding to feedback in Instagram comments, RiseUp admitted they focused on "women and girls" and referred to trans and non-binary folks getting abortions as "others" (we have screenshots).

RevCom also has a homophobic past. Up until 2002, the group's official position was that homosexuality contributed to women's oppression, amongst other nonsense. While RevCom and its fronts have since begun to include platitudes for the rights of LGBTQ+ peoples, they have yet to apologize for this past or issue a statement or position in defense LGBTQ+ rights.

RiseUp continues to intentionally exclude sex workers.

Sunsara Taylor, the brain behind RiseUp's grift, is explicitly against sex work and the porn industry (see her prior activism with Stop Patriarchy). Sunsara Taylor's stance is harmful to the fight for abortion, which we believe must be intersectional.

We urge everyone to share this message widely to prevent fellow organizers and friends from getting further involved with RiseUp and its affiliated fronts.

How to answer an attack on a movement I co-initiated, with whom I shared so much of my experience and strategic thinking? I had gotten a whiff of this thinking when I wrote individually to a few people who had sent in scathing critical letters to RiseUp. They were absolutely convinced that Sunsara was a modern Mephistopheles and anyone who worked with her was just as evil. As I realized I could not make a case with anyone I had spoken to, and after reading these ridiculous and scurrilous "charges," especially the part of Sunsara being the "brain"—what were Lori and I?—I decided that a legal letter might give them pause.

Our attorneys sent cease-and-desist letters to the following organizations: Reproductive Justice Collective, United Against Racism & Fascism NYC, Shout Your Abortion Washington Square Park Mutual Aid, Mujeres en Resistancia NY:NJ, Abortion Access Front, The Jane Fund, Reproductive Rights Coalition, Chicago Abortion Fund, SWOP Brooklyn, Forward Midwifery, New Mexico Religious Coalition for Reproductive Choice, Abortion Access Nashville, Buckle Business Fund, Women's Information Network of NYC (WIN. NYC), National Institute of Reproductive Health Action Fund.

"It has come to RiseUp's attention that your organization has added its named as a signatory to the Statement," the letter read. "Be advised that we have sent the attached cease and desist letter to NYC for Abortion Rights demanding that they remove the Statement due to its defamatory and inaccurate content. Since you are a signatory to the Statement, we are sharing the cease and desist letter with you so that you are aware you have signed on to a Statement not based in truth, that could potentially be subject to litigation."

We also put out a statement immediately:

To Those Who Would Rather Lie, Slander, and Attack RiseUp4AbortionRights Than Unite All Who Can Be United Against This Fascist Assault,

On the very day that women in multiple states will now be faced with the terrifying life-threatening consequences of abortion bans—these groups choose to attack the only group that has been calling for sustained nonviolent struggle and protests to stop this since January! RiseUp4AbortionRights has consistently, since its formation, called for the broadest possible united action, in the streets, against what was then the looming

Supreme Court decision ripping away abortion rights. Read the actual founding statement of RiseUp4AbortionRights and see whether it comports with what its accusers claim. The sad fact is that the great bulk of the "reproductive rights movement" chose to downplay the severity of the attack. They simultaneously counseled people to prepare for a "post-Roe" America rather than throw everything into preventing the decision. Many of these organizations attacked RiseUp for saying that this assault on abortion was overwhelmingly focused on women, even as RiseUp also spoke out against the way this assault would be used against the rights of LGBTQ+ people (as can already be seen in Clarence Thomas's concurring opinion yesterday) and consistently pointed to the disproportionate effect the overturning of *Roe* would have on Black and Latina women, and other women of color.

We urged all activists to "focus their efforts on struggling to reverse this attack on the fundamental right to abortion and not squander precious time and unity fomenting unprincipled attacks on groups and individuals that have been fighting for abortion rights and providing abortion care for years."

We wanted to unite. But the response was strong: "No way." I wasn't aware of it at the time, but many of the grassroots players of what existed of the pro-choice movement were in lockstep with Planned Parenthood and the Democratic Party. They, too, had been getting ready for *Dobbs*. As soon as it happened, the funding vehicles to raise money for women to travel to "safe states" were already in place. It reminded me of when I was demonstrating with Bill Baird in Ohio. A couple of the Antis came up to me and said, "You are hurting women. You are working against women." The idea that the work that I had dedicated my life to, and now the work I was doing with RiseUp, would hurt women was abhorrent to me.

After *Dobbs*, we were considered to be taking money away from women. There were some who believed that by *not* funding travel, we were actively hurting women—that we were misdirecting those funds away from the nonprofits, and passively hurting people by presenting ourselves as an authentic radical group. I have the dubious honor of having been attacked as a Communist cult follower *and* as a capitalist making money off of the movement!

The fact that I ran a for-profit clinic did not stop many individuals and organizations from coming to me for funding, which I usually gave them from my nonprofit, Diana Foundation. All the funds raised were put back into the movement. There is and was a negative judgment about the fact that I was a radical feminist, writer, and activist—but one who had a "for-profit" clinic.

But the difference between a for-profit and a nonprofit organization is primarily in the accounting and in the regulations dictating where nonprofits can spend money. A part of the reason these groups were so against RiseUp is that *all* organizations are competing for funds. They were concerned we were taking money not from the patients, but from the other organizations. There was no understanding of the fact that designating an organization a "nonprofit" was more an accounting and tax paradigm than a transparent description of the way "profits" were utilized.

The Democratic Party and Planned Parenthood, with the support of all the nonprofits, were setting the agenda. The agenda was to raise money for distribution of the abortion pills and to help women travel to states where abortions were accessible. They did not want an uprising. They felt that anything radical would get in the way. They didn't want girls acting up. They wanted us to be good and quiet. But didn't they know that "good girls never make history"? It was so similar to when the Women's March put out a statement that the participants could not dress as "handmaids" or bring hangers.

These groups wanted to take us out, particularly Sunsara because of her connection to Bob Avakian and the Revolutionary Communist Party. When the attacks on Sunsara began, people said I should cut her loose. But I felt I had a responsibility to a sister-in-arms. And besides, did they think that she would ruin my "bad" reputation? Together, we were accused of vicious things. This was really the first time I was attacked by association.

The depth and cruelty of the attacks—the lies and slanders—were a huge surprise to me. I've been attacked many, many times throughout my life. (As I mentioned earlier, I was even called Hitler on national television.) But not with such lies, not with such blatant propaganda, and not from the people that were supposed to be on my side! The truth is what people want to believe, not what's actually true, so it becomes increasingly difficult to fight. For the first time, I was forced to defend a colleague's personal financial and political history. It was akin to the attacks on political candidates' children or spouses. The worst part was that it placed me personally into a derivative group identity and spilled over to RiseUp itself.

I'm aware of all the propaganda out there. The attacks were meant to bring us down by using smear tactics and putting us on the defensive to ultimately just get us out of their way. There was a large national pro-choice meeting at one point, and we were told, in so many words, that we were not welcome in their pro-choice space. (The exact language was that we were "not welcome [at the Women's Convention in Houston] and we were not given permission to attend.") We were heretics! And we had to be excised from the body politic. There could be no debate or discussion. But we resisted and continued to make our points and eventually they "allowed" us to have a space at the conference. (In the end the organization that rejected us managed to find enough integrity to do the right thing and allow us to attend and present our materials.)

Worst of all, a few of the young people involved with RiseUp sent us letters saying that they could not continue to work with anyone associated with Stop Patriarchy or REVCOM (two activist groups that work with RiseUp). This was a major eye-opener for me. There was no curiosity or desire to find out the truth of these accusations—I was made to feel like an outcast by the people I was, in theory, working *with* in pursuit of a shared goal. But in practice, they considered us heretical.

Of course, I'd seen infighting before, but the public nature of these attacks was new for me. And there was a very unified front.

Jezebel, of all places, published an article in which they called us a "problematic group," among other things.[36]

"The group's strategy across the country has been to stage shocking spectacles to ignite outrage and action. And while the shock value certainly seemed to work, garnering national attention and tweets of support, the productivity of such displays, especially when put on by a group like this one, is murky at best," the article read.

> In April, after the Kentucky legislature effectively ended legal abortion in the state, Jezebel reported that RiseUp4AbortionRights was organizing a day of action and calling for volunteers to distribute wire coat hangers with its fliers nationwide during something they called "National Coat Hanger Day," complete with "die-ins in bloody gowns that dramatize the nightmare this will mean for women." At the time, *Jezebel* pointed out that these tactics wouldn't actually help Kentuckians get abortions and that the group's theatrics might've actually taken resources from local grassroots organizations and abortion funds.
>
> "Kentucky-based organizers have been quite clear they don't want RiseUp4AbortionRights descending on their communities," Erin Matson, co-founder and executive director of Reproaction, had told us. As for the coat hangers? *Jezebel*'s Susan Rinkunas pointed out that coat hangers as symbols for the abortion rights movement are both controversial and confusing, as they suggest that all illegal abortions are unsafe and do little to acknowledge the safety of a self-managed abortion with abortion pills.
>
> . . .
>
> Speaking of enslaved! RiseUp4AbortionRights has proudly touted the chant "FORCED MOTHERHOOD IS FEMALE ENSLAVEMENT" across their branded platforms. For starters, the use of "enslavement" feels . . . inappropriate given that the leaders of this group are not Black. Then, while forcing people

---

36 Emily Leibert, "Topless Abortion Activists Who Stormed a WNBA Game Are Part of Problematic Group," *Jezebel*, June 8, 2022, https://jezebel.com/topless-abortion -activists-who-stormed-a-wnba-game-are-1849035472.

to give birth is an affront to human rights, the repeated usage of gendered terms in this repeated warcry excludes trans and nonbinary pregnant people who need abortion access and care. As the cherry on top, the group's green scarves are an appropriation of the "Marea Verde" or "Green Wave" that, according to Refinery29, first emerged in Argentina over a decade ago as activists there fought to decriminalize abortion, though they are far from the only abortion rights group to use them.

Worse, *Jezebel* refused to print our full response:

In response to Emily Leibert's June 8th commentary at *Jezebel* entitled, "Topless Abortion Activists Who Stormed WNBA Game Are Part of Problematic Group," as co-initiators of the organization responsible for this protest, RiseUp4AbortionRights, we take issue with many of her negative claims about our organization's purpose and strategy. We cannot determine whether Ms. Leibert was unable to truly understand our mission, has not taken the time to read our many public statements, or simply refuses to see facts beyond her own veil of prejudice.

She cites so many misleading and misinformed points, it is difficult to know where to start, so we'll start at the very bottom, where we believe the core problem emanates.

The article's final line conveys extreme hopelessness, as reflected in its declaration that "the cards have already been played, and *Roe* is about to tumble." Had we not known that this article was written by a feminist for a feminist publication, we might have thought it was written by an extreme anti-abortion activist. What is the benefit of making such a discouraging claim, unless to dampen the intentions of all pro-abortion activists, encouraging them to step back, sit down, and do nothing to try to stop the Supreme Court from overturning *Roe* without a fight? Is that what she really wants?

Speaking about "cards," let's put all of our cards on the table. How did we all end up in this position where the basic right of half of society to determine their own reproduction, lives and destinies is on track to be obliterated? We got here because the Democratic Party and all too many pro-choice organizations and people continually compromised for decades when attacks were made on abortion access and anti-abortion legislation. Again and again, they minimized the tenacity and commitment of the opposition and refused to stand up in massive, disruptive protest to draw a firm line and say, "NO MORE!" This, along with the constant desire to "talk across the aisle," while throwing Black and poor women under the bus by failing to strongly, publicly and collectively oppose the Hyde Amendment, was a strong message from our side that a "little" invasion of women's bodies and their rights were just fine.

History has repeatedly shown that disruptive protests are often the only way to achieve change. Recall Alice Paul who, in 1913, led the Suffrage Movement by marching down Pennsylvania Avenue, past the White House, even while being assaulted and attacked. As a result, public outrage led to wider support for the suffrage movement.

We are also inspired by how RiseUp activist Guido Reichstadter was arrested [. . .] after he hopped over the barricades outside the Supreme Court and chained himself to the fence, elevating the Green Bandana of abortion rights.

As for Ms. Leibert's accusation that we have somehow wrongly "appropriated" this powerful symbol from women in Latin American, let us quote one of the comments left by a reader of her article: "What's wrong with using the colors from another successful pro-abortion rights group? ... This isn't Fendi selling fucking [N]ative [A]merican headdresses as fashion; its international political solidarity." We have been tremendously strengthened by the example of, as well as the direct messages of, solidarity we have received from activists in Argentina, Colombia, Mexico, and other parts of the world.

But because Ms. Leibert gave us this gift, even if inadvertently, we will give her one as well. We agree that donating to abortion funds can be helpful, as asserted in her article. But to quote her own subheading, "That's only half the story," it is

Bill Baird displaying his presentation of household instruments that women would use to self-abort when abortion was illegal. Pro-Choice Rally in Union Square, New York City, April 29th, 1988. (Published by permission of Gary O'Neil; Bettye Lane Photographs, Rubenstein Rare Book & Manuscript Library, Duke University)

Bill Baird, Merle Hoffman, Carolyn Handel. March on 5th Avenue, New York City, April 1988. (Published by permission of Gary O'Neil; Bettye Lane Photographs, Rubenstein Rare Book & Manuscript Library, Duke University)

RiseUp4AbortionRights.org

LEGAL ABORTION ON DEMAND & WITHOUT APOLOGY NATIONWIDE

Grace Paley speaking at podium; Merle Hoffman and Bill Baird (behind).
Pro-Choice Rally in Union Square, New York City, April 29th, 1988.
(Published by permission of Gary O'Neil; Bettye Lane Photographs,
Rubenstein Rare Book & Manuscript Library, Duke University)

Merle Hoffman visits supporters in front of Choices Women's Medical Center.
Queens, New York. (Published by permission of Joan L. Roth)

Merle Hoffman and activists holding photos of individuals who died from botched illegal abortions outside St. Patrick's Cathedral, right before stopping traffic in the middle of 5th Avenue. RiseUp's First Act of Civil Disobedience. New York City, February 27th, 2022. (Published by permission of Joan L. Roth)

Antis outside the Supreme Court. Washington, DC.
(Published by permission of Joan L. Roth)

*Escort and supporter in front of Choices Women's Medical Center opposing
the Antis across the street with Dr. George Tiller's words. Queens, New York.*
(Published by permission of Joan L. Roth)

*Anti-choice protester outside of Choices Women's Medical Center.
Queens, New York.* (Published by permission of Joan L. Roth)

RiseUp4AbortionRights.org

NOT ONE MORE

DOCTOR SCARED TO PERFORM LIFE SAVING CARE

Guido Reichstadter in front of the Supreme Court prior to his arrest.
(Published by permission of Ford Fischer/News2Share)

RiseUp4AbortionRights rally. (Published by permission of
RightUp4AbortionRights.org)

Die-In Protest at Cathedral of Christ the King Church. Atlanta, Mother's Day 2022.
(Published by permission of RiseUp4AbortionRights.org)

important to understand that simply sending money to abortion funds is not a long-term or comprehensive solution. Millions of women are going to need abortions if *Roe* is overturned, and abortion supporters are not going to be able to pay for all of them. Many very young women, women in prisons and detention, women who lack legal documents, women trapped in abuse and other dangerous situations will be beyond the reach of even the most resourceful and committed networks of support. Many trans and non-binary people who need abortions will be, too. Further, the fines for "aiding and abetting," not to mention paying the price of potential jail terms for doing so, will only lead to paying at least double for our oppression.

Will it be easy to stop the Supreme Court from turning its draft into law? No.

But there are millions and millions of us whose health, safety and futures will be impacted, and it would be unconscionable not to fight with all we've got while we've still got a chance. As we recently wrote in our Call to Come to DC, starting on Monday, June 13: "Even fascist women-haters worry about losing the perceived legitimacy of their institutions and their system when they are faced with truly massive, un-ignorable and unrelenting nonviolent resistance. And, if even in the face of our determined opposition, the Court still revokes abortion rights, we will be in a far stronger position to continue the struggle for women's freedom for having dared to RISE UP!"

To close, we will quote just one more of the dozens of people who responded to your article by dismissing many of its points: *"Can you point to a protest that, in and of itself, was capable of enacting legal change, or are all protests worthless?"* We will not apologize for risking our safety to stand up for women's fundamental rights. For it is, in fact, stated in one of our most prominent slogans: Abortion On Demand And Without Apology!

They should have been strategizing, working with anybody out there who could help. But they had to get us out of the game.

The question is why they had to exclude us. One could easily say it was "mean girl behavior" motivated by envy, a sense of competition, and feelings of shame that they were not in the limelight. They tried to put some kind of moral, political, virtuous skin on actions that from my point of view were craven and selfish. This was made even worse by defining them as moral and just.

I was very invested in RiseUp. Yes, there were issues. Yes, there were problems, but I'm very proud of the work that was done and of what we accomplished.

CHAPTER 7
RESISTANCE AND REVOLUTION

Loss

When I was first asked how I felt about the *Dobbs* decision, I compared it to the death of my mother. More than ten years earlier, when my mother had been diagnosed with terminal dementia, and I was told her brain was shrinking, I knew it was only going to get worse—physically, physiologically, and psychologically.

When she was finally bedridden, I recognized that she was in the initial stages of dying. By that point, I was helping diaper her, combing her thinning hair, and holding her like a baby. It was the most intimate time I ever spent with her. And there was laughter also. She could be wonderfully sarcastic. At one point I said I had to leave, and she replied, "What? Do you have a date?" Another time she looked straight at me and said, "Well I suppose, everyone has to die some time."

Through those final stages, as she was screaming and throwing her hands up in pain, she called out the names of old, long-dead friends. With her favorite Chopin waltzes playing in the background, she looked and sounded as if she were being tortured. I asked the doctor if he thought she was in pain even with the morphine he was giving her. He said he didn't think so. But she could not express her inner experiences.

She didn't stop screaming. It was horrible. The doctors said to me, "The level of morphine we'd have to give your mother . . . she won't come out of it." I don't think I thought about it for very long. Or maybe I had already thought about it. "Please, give it to her," I told them.

I was right there, talking to her, as that last dose was administered. I was watching her live her last moments. The medical assistant in the room said, "Her feet are starting to marble," and silently together we watched the work of death—that final mystery that comes for all of us. I simply sat there breathing with her. Her breath would come and go. I breathed along with her, just as I had with so many patients over the years. I'd think that was the last one, but then there was another. It was a long process, but then, finally, it was all over.

A second ago she was alive, and now she isn't, I thought. But the difference between knowing that death is coming and trying to prepare for it, and the reality of it is a black hole whose gravitational pull drags you to a depth you can't imagine until you live inside of it.

Likewise, I was prepared for *Dobbs*, for the eventuality of *Roe* being overturned. I knew it was coming. Still, I hoped it wouldn't be as bad as I knew it would be. I *thought* I was ready for it. But in the end, it was a death like any other—impossible to prepare for—and the loss was far greater than anything I could have imagined. The question becomes how to deal with that loss, how to grieve it. Death is a frightening reality for most people and we as a society have a very hard time dealing with it. I've thought about death since I was a little girl and I studied it through philosophy throughout my life. The ancients spoke of having to *practice* dying. Heraclitus said you never step into the same river twice; life is always changing through loss and new beginnings. I had been practicing this philosophy from a very young age.

Grief

The psychiatrist Elisabeth Kubler-Ross, a pioneer in thinking about how people mourn, gave us five (and later seven) stages of grief. She offered a road map of sorts. First, there is shock, then denial, followed by anger, bargaining, depression, testing, and finally acceptance. I saw a great many people moving through these stages after *Dobbs*, including myself.

Shock. Kamala Harris declared herself "shocked" by the *Dobbs* decision. She wasn't alone. So many people were shocked because they had not been reading the signs, so many of which had been blazing red and right in front of us for years.

Denial. Denial was operative even after the leak. People "just couldn't believe" what was happening. And denial was the default for so many decades as we lived through the assault on *Roe*. There was always the belief, even as Antis chipped away at abortion rights over the years, that *Roe* would/could not be overturned.

Anger. There were many people who said things like "how could they? How dare they?" with something resembling righteous anger. But they could, and they dared. Publicly and globally, the only real expression of anger right after the decision in front of the Supreme Court was coming from RiseUp. We stood there in defiance, shouting our slogans. Everyone else on our side was crying and hugging each other.

Bargaining. I don't believe that there was any bargaining going on at all. To bargain, each side must have some type of leverage, and our side had absolutely none unless we went full frontal into magical thinking and relied solely on voting as the main tactic (which is exactly what happened).

Depression. Many people, including many activists, described themselves as being "depressed." Depression leads to despair. The loss of *Roe* has made many people question their own judgment and the meaning of all their past activism.

Testing. We didn't have to wait long for this one. It was one or two weeks after the decision that the case of a ten-year-old-girl who was raped ran up against the heartbeat bill in Texas.

Acceptance. Unfortunately, this is the stage in which most of us are living now. I would propose that we cannot allow this to happen.

We have to replace acceptance with anger, which in turn must fuel the long-term strategic, tactical responses to this situation. Death is unavoidable, but *this* is not.

When you lose a parent, a loved one, or a friend, anger is a huge part of the grieving process. People may not recognize it as such, and one is not supposed to get angry. But anger is natural, and anger is beneficial. How can you not be angry? You've been abandoned: "How could they leave me like this? Someone they loved."

There was a great deal of rage after *Dobbs*. But what to do with that rage? It can be a great motivator, but it must be controlled and directed. You can't simply sit back and say, "fuck the government, fuck these people, fuck the opposition." That is anger, but it is unharnessed anger. And you can't keep it inside either, or you will fall into despair. This is very common with women because in our society to be an angry woman is a very bad thing. Women are supposed to be nice, to be "good girls."

I say we must lean into our anger. We have to feel it and name it for what it is. And then, we must use our anger as sacred fuel. If you are not angry at being thrust into the position of second-class citizenship, there is something radically wrong. We must also ask what it means to "accept" the death of *Roe*. We must make a distinction between acceptance and normalization. I accept the *Dobbs* decision because I have no choice, but I don't accept the loss it has led to.

Mourn for Five Minutes. Then Organize.

The movement, however, was very quick to accept the *Dobbs* decision. They were resigned to it. "There was nothing we could do," I heard people say. I disagreed, which is why with RiseUp, I went out in the beginning to stop the Supreme Court decision. It was a one-in-a-million chance, but you have to get up and make an attempt. This is the power and courage of No. This is resistance.

I'll have this anger as long as I live. People have told me, "You're so passionate, you're so intense. Where does that come from?" It comes from the confidence and the belief in what I know is true, the necessity of my believing that I have to speak that truth and act on that truth. It comes from my belief in the power of resistance. I can understand that so many people would view RiseUp's attempt to stop the Supreme Court from overturning *Roe* as a quixotic attempt. Even I thought it was impossible. But, as we wrote in our statement:

> It is of great political and historical importance that RiseUp4AbortionRights united people from very diverse political perspectives and unleashed the fury of tens of thousands of young women and many others in mass nonviolent action with the aim of stopping the Supreme Court from overturning *Roe*.
>
> In the end, the fight to save *Roe* did not reach the size, determination, or unity needed to win. But we modeled courage, inspired millions, and dared to speak the truth about what this rollback is really about.

Defining Resistance and the Courage of No

Before resistance there has to be an acknowledgment of the reality, then integration into consciousness, then a decision about "rightness." If one comes to the conclusion that something is "not right" or "not fair," resistance is the courage of saying "no" and acting on it. Resistance is action.

The self is born in resistance. And the creation of the self defines its boundaries in the struggle and the negotiation with others. If you do not push against something that pushes or binds you, there is no tension. There can be no self.

Children are natural resistance fighters. They do not discriminate against particular types of authority, but understand organically that all power can, and in some cases must, be resisted. Yet, as a child moves into the communal reality, they lose the other parts of being a child—wonder, awe, gratitude, and whimsy. Children see the world without definition. They look at what we have named a tree and are amazed at the height, the different colored leaves or flowers, or the exquisite blue of the sky at sunset, the fullness of the moon. I have tried not to lose that childlike sense of wonder. I go so far as to make a point of cherishing it. There is a trust in my own imagination, which is another part of ourselves that gets co-opted by ideology. Imagination is occupied by screen representations of "reality."

One could almost say that education consists of the slow, relentless process of learning to assent and to conform—the disenchantment of the world. While a certain amount of conformity is necessary for any society to exist and survive (stopping at red lights, for example), in both fundamentalist and fascist societies the very notion of an individual self becomes redefined and authenticated through its immersion in the group ideology. Individualism is rooted out and rote is reinforced.

Whether it is the "yes, sir, no, sir" salutes or the chanting of the leaders' great words, the teaching of youth to follow in lockstep is a goal of every right-wing entity. The natural obstacle of this coerced uniformity is freethinking and independence, fueled by creativity and imagination of the possible. Critical thinking, doubt, and questioning are the enemies of groupthink.

In tightly controlled societies, those who are too independent are considered heretics. They are burned at the stake, stoned to death, or beheaded for refusing to engage in what seems to be an esoteric debate or a matter of style, such as not agreeing with the Catholic belief in the infallibility of the Pope and the existence of purgatory—two main differences from the Protestant faith—but insisting that it comes from faith alone. These practices were everyday realities during the religious wars of the Reformation in the mid-sixteenth century as well as during the Spanish Inquisition. In fact, the very meaning of heresy is "an opinion, doctrine, or practice contrary to the truth or to generally accepted beliefs or standards."

The de-platforming, academic firings, and shunning of those who do not conform to the current "woke" ideology and creed is an example of how we deal with heretics today. While there are no beheadings in the public squares, there is certainly de-platforming, shunning, and social death for those who refuse to conform.

Actually, wokeism goes even further by attacking the dead and rewriting or wanting to erase history.

How is it, then, that there are those who can resist; those who doubt, question, and discover the truths behind manipulated collective reality; who turn their insights and denial into action, and have the courage to go up against the status quo, sometimes at the cost of their own lives? Are those who resist able to retain some of that childlike ability to see reality before the weight of accepted definitions closes their eyes and mind, to see through surfaces to the essence of the thing itself, apart from immediate representations? Are they able to recognize the hypocrisy and myopia that are bars to independence and freedom in the same way that a brilliant physicist constructs a new scientific theory after observing daily phenomena like an apple falling or a ball rolling?

There was always the enchantment of resistance growing up, which drew me to characters like Joan of Arc from a very young age. I also grew up with stories of my Aunt Natasha and Uncle Vuluga. In the late nineteenth century, they were part of a Russian terrorist group called Narodnaya Volya (People's Will), best known for multiple attempts on Czar Alexander II's life. The group was ultimately successful, and Natasha and Vuluga, who had planned many of the actions, were caught, tried for treason, and sent to a labor camp in Siberia for life. Somehow, they managed to escape and make their way across many miles of the snow-covered Siberian steppe to settle in Staten Island, New York. Audacious and courageous, they put their lives on the line for a cause. (I met them only once and the memory of that meeting formed the beginning of my memoir *Intimate Wars*.) Those were models I could point to and say, "those people were singular individuals. They followed their own voice." But they lived in a time where one could *hear* and potentially *listen* to their own voices. (Now our ears and attention are full of screaming opinion makers and influencers.)

In his book, *Empire of Illusion: The End of Literacy and the Triumph of Spectacle*, the Pulitzer Prize–winning author, war journalist, and seminarian Chris Hedges presents a scathing critique of the coarsening and deadening of American society, calling it a "necrophiliac" culture. He describes a population so transfixed by media glitz and celebrity that it has lost its independent thinking ability and moral compass. While Hedges does say that resistance is a "moral imperative and sustains a life of meaning," he strongly believes that power is inherently corrupt. He writes that it is unrealistic to expect good people to rule, echoing the words of Robespierre who notably said during the French Revolution, "No power rules innocently."

It is our moral imperative, I believe, to resist by recognizing and dismantling the opposition's "outposts in our heads" with the understanding that it is biological women who can give life—a wonderful, difficult, and massive responsibility. With the current ability to control and plan our reproduction, I view this as an individual moral decision, not as a decision to be defined by the power structure of the Supreme Court, the state, the church, the patriarchy—no, this decision must rest with each individual. The first part of resistance is the knowledge of this truth. When we integrate that truth into our very consciousness, then resistance should come naturally.

We live in a time in which everything has become political in a "me-them" paradigm: red-blue, right-left. But political resistance can't simply be found in the voting booth. Nothing within the electoral system can be considered political resistance. Politics is about compromise, and resistance has to be uncompromising. You must operate outside of the existing structure. One must put out a vision and be ready to pay a price.

But perhaps the real question is: can any national nonprofit organization operate as a resistance to government policies when they are increasingly dependent on federal funding? A prime example is Planned Parenthood's resistance to joining RiseUp in some actions because, in their words, they were "not a single-issue organization." They positioned themselves exactly as a single-issue organization when they are presenting as the voice of the pro-choice movement or influencing groups such as the Women's March, who parrot their anxiety about the "hanger" issue.

Planned Parenthood had used the rhetoric of radicals like me and radical actions like mine for decades. They would use some of the verbiage and fundraise off of it. However, when it came to working together, they would distance themselves.

There are, of course, limits on what nonprofits can do as agents of resistance. They have to answer to boards, to their funders, to their published mission, to the IRS, and to regulators. Understandably, they may not want their activists to take off their tops in church. But instead of supporting the organized attack against us, they could have acknowledged that we were shining a light on the struggle. If they don't have the organizational courage to show respect for differences and discuss them among ourselves, they can at least refrain from being silent during the outrageous attacks that we faced.

Many times throughout my career I have had difficulties with and left the very organizations that I played a part in creating and building. Some friction may have been due to my wanting to hold onto my original vision, but often it had to do with the fact of new people coming in and committing the political matricide necessary to do what *they* wanted to do. They had to push the mothers out of the picture. I've even been attacked by those organizations in the process.

I recall at one of the NAF conferences noticing signs for the Latina Caucus and the Black Women's Caucus. And then I saw a sign for the Feminist Caucus. I went to the caucus and made a statement explaining that if the organization considered feminism a topic of caucusing, then it was no longer the feminist organization I founded nor one I want to continue to be a part of. I left the room and the organization.

I also left NCAP over their handling of the Ron Fitzsimmons fiasco. Fitzsimmons, then the executive director of NCAP, had lied ("intentionally misled," in his words) in his statements on second-trimester abortions "because he feared that the truth would damage the cause of abortion rights." In an interview with the *New York Times*, he said he "lied through his teeth" when he had gone on *Nightline* and said the procedure was used rarely.[37]

---

37 David Stout, "An Abortion Rights Advocate Says He Lied About Procedure," *New York Times*, February 27, 1997, https://www.nytimes.com/1997/02/26/us/an-abortion-rights-advocate-says-he-lied-about-procedure.html.

Fitzsimmons did immeasurable damage to both the organization and to the movement. I strongly believed that he should have resigned and that the board should have demanded it. All of the other women involved insisted he be given a second chance. I felt I had no choice but to leave the organization. (As of this writing, I am again working closely with NAF.)

The Activism of the 1960s and 1970s

During a period of great upheaval, mainly as a result of the Vietnam War, many people came of age politically, myself included. Young people were taking risks to resist. They were burning draft cards, putting themselves on the line. There are still many lessons we can learn from the activism of that era.

On May 4, 1970, the Ohio National Guard opened fire on students holding a peaceful rally at Kent State University. Twenty-eight soldiers fired sixty-seven rounds in thirteen seconds, killing four students. It was an unspeakable tragedy, and it sparked a massive wave of anti-war uprisings across the country. I was in college at the time, but I was several years older than everyone else since I took time to study music in Paris. I was aware of the political climate, but I was interested in other things. I was focused on working three jobs and getting through school.

There was quite a lot of activism at Queens College, and like many students, I was deeply impacted by the murder of those students in Ohio. I remember very distinctly sitting in a Psychology of Personality class when someone came in, picked up the microphone, and said, "I'm liberating this microphone. Everybody should walk out of the room and join the demonstrations outside."

"That's fine," the professor said. "Everyone can leave, but if you leave, no one in this class will get a grade." He knew we all wanted to get into graduate school, and you couldn't go without that grade. Everyone got up and left except me. I believed him. I made a calculation, since I wanted to go to graduate school and I needed that grade. I wasn't going to throw that away to march around and place papier-mâché gravestones on the ground. In the end, it didn't matter at all. No one was punished. All classes were given a pass/mark that semester. I resented the fact that I had worked hard and wanted my work to be acknowledged. There was no price to pay, and that made a lasting impression on me. I realized I could never automatically believe those in positions of authority. My decisions had to be my own and no one else's.

There was another incident at Queens College that also left an impression on me. I was almost finished with classes when my father died. The grade in my Industrial Psychology course was to be based on three major exams and two papers. I had completed everything but the final paper and was on track to earn an A. I requested the professor consider my circumstances and give the grade I had largely already earned, but he refused and required me to do the paper over summer break. I had no choice but to agree. With all the trauma and difficulty of that summer, I wrote thirty pages. This professor had made an arrangement with me to meet me at the school prior to when official classes started. I remember walking up to his office and confidently placing the paper on his desk.

"Thank you," he said, flipping through the pages. "Now I can give you your grade."

"Aren't you going to read it?" I asked.

"No," he replied. "I just wanted to ensure that you completed it."

This was a small interaction, but a huge lesson about the arbitrary nature of power. It is one I've carried with me all these years.

In that era, the war in Vietnam produced a great sense of urgency. People were being killed every day—the war was on the evening news. No one could ignore it. I believe the pro-choice movement has lost that urgency. We have lost that rage. I knew it was lost when a lot of the major pro-choice organizations were already planning for the fall of *Roe*. They surrendered before it was even over.

When you have organizations like Planned Parenthood and the Women's March that want to distance themselves from the very nature of the reality of the results of illegal abortion by not showing coat hangers and by not allowing costumes of handmaidens, we are censoring the deaths of women and the dangers of illegal abortion. These deaths are no longer viewed as casualties of the war against women but as terribly sad individual events.

So many minority groups understand and present themselves as a class, a community, an organized interest group. Yet, women resist this because of the outposts in their heads, the fear of appropriation, the resistance to seeking a transcendent definition of "woman" that goes beyond geography, race, and culture and gender identity. At this point, the need for this definition is even greater when there is a hot culture battle going on in this country about the primary definition of "woman."

Perhaps it is our unrealistic expectations of what fighting for a cause actually means that need adjustment. We may not have victory in our lifetimes, but it is the struggle against oppression and the struggle toward freedom that is the achievement. The many victories that have been won along with all setbacks—and the depression and even despair that can accompany them—are pit stops along the way.

Many years ago, I did an interview with Petra Kelly, founder of the West German Green Party and an anti-nuclear activist. She said there are "many moments where I more or less fold up, moments when my head says stop but my heart keeps going." That is where we have to look for courage: to the heart of the actor, the heart of the person. Antonio Gramsci, an Italian writer, politician, and theorist of the early twentieth century who was imprisoned by Mussolini's Fascist regime, wrote: "I'm a pessimist because of intelligence, but an optimist because of will."

The illusion of the pro-choice movement is that there is one battle that can be won, and our struggle will be over for all time; that there will be a final retreat of the desire to exercise power or to control women; that reproductive freedom will, alone among freedoms, stand rock solid without ever facing the pressure of forces that want to contain it.

Looking at the 1960s, one wonders if the era of mass politics is over. Yet the Black Lives Matter movement offers some hope for the power of uncompromising persistence. Of course, there were some performative aspects of the BLM protests—but the movement has largely resisted calls to normalize, compromise, or capitulate. Standing in stark contrast is the pro-choice movement. That is why it is imperative to continue to keep the goal of legal abortion nationwide front and center and to always remind people that "as long as one woman is not free—none of us are free."

Loving the Struggle

We are living in a post-truth, post-clarity world in which everything is a "social construct." To me, this is merely an excuse for non-action and group-think. Yes, it is possible—easy, even—to look at our current situation and say, "Everything is confusing. What could I do?" But that is only true if you depend on the narratives set out for you by political parties, ideologies, and religions.

If you understand one basic truth—that women are second-class citizens without the fundamental right to a legal, safe abortion nationwide—there is clarity. If you understand the nature of reproductive justice, there can be no confusion. There is no chaos. There is a pure laser focus on the truth. If you are angry, you don't get to sit this out and say, "Well, I'm still not sure." As Frederick Douglass once eloquently put it: "Those who profess to favor freedom and yet deprecate agitation are men who want crops without plowing up the ground; they want rain without thunder and lightning. They want the ocean without the awful roar of its many waters. This struggle may be a moral one, or it may be a physical one, and it may be both moral and physical, but it must be a struggle. Power concedes nothing without a demand. It never did and it never will."

One may not be sure how they can act, but we have to understand the reality of non-action. My old friend Flo Kennedy used to say we must "learn to love the struggle," a kind of love that will sustain a life of meaning. I once heard Flo speak at Queens College. She was the first Black woman to graduate from Harvard Law

School. She was a well-known radical and when she spoke, it was prophetic: "If men could have abortions, it would be a sacrament."

We became very good friends over the years, and it was from Flo (and from Camus's *Myth of Sisyphus*—always pushing that enormous rock back up the hill) that I learned a different definition of love.

It was Camus who wrote, in the last lines of *Sisyphus*, that "one must imagine Sisyphus happy." He is not a victim. He is happy because he has a purpose. He keeps going. His rock rolls down the hill and he pushes it up again and again and again. This idea is embedded very deeply in me. We will never get to a point where there is no opposition.

In the fall of 1994, I, along with Andrea Dworkin, spoke with the late Congressman John Lewis about what it means to resist. Congressman Lewis was an extraordinary figure in the struggle for civil rights. But he was not my choice to interview. Andrea Dworkin was a friend of mine and a contributor to *On the Issues*. One day we were sitting in an Afghan restaurant talking about the people we admire. I asked if she could sit down with anyone for a conversation, who it would be? She immediately said John Lewis. I arranged for both of us to go to Washington and speak with him.

Speaking with John, I found a person with an immense sense of humanity. He had suffered. He was someone who never stopped putting everything on the line, but his anger never turned to bitterness or resentment. In our conversation, it was clear that he was grappling with what Andrea really wanted to address—violence against women.

The conversation ultimately turned into a discussion of passive resistance.

John Lewis: Why is it that all at once we are facing so much violence in this society? I really believe that in our own country, the greatest need is for a revolution of values—a revolution in the minds and hearts of people. I happen to believe that in every human being there is a spark of something that is greater than any of us. No one has the right to abuse or destroy that divine spark. But it's not just hitting someone. The way you look at someone or stare also can be damaging and hurtful. That's why I believe in the philosophy of nonviolence, not simply as a technique but as a way of life. The end must be caught up in the means. You cannot separate the two.

Andrea Dworkin: For me, this is a question of tremendous personal moral crisis. In the last ten years, I have had a real crisis around this issue of violence, and I can't come to terms with it. I see women being raped on a level of frequency and with a kind of sadism that is increasingly horrible. And I see women being beaten in their own homes, so that for us it's not even a question of "Are the streets safe?" because most of us are killed in our own homes. And I see an almost complete devaluation of the worth of women—on the marketplace, through pornography, through prostitution, and an attitude that women are almost subhuman—and a belief that men seem to have that they have a right to control women, to control access to women's bodies, on a visceral level. It has become impossible for me to tolerate the way the law is not working for women, not operating on behalf of women.

I have come to believe that the only way to stop a rapist, a wife beater, may be to kill him. If the society does not react to the violence that women experience as if it's an emergency, then a woman has to find a way to stop that man herself. When you look at violence against women, you find that most of it is in the circle of those close relationships, in an environment that we call love.

Lewis: Yes. I have seen it firsthand. When I was growing up, I had an uncle who was the meanest man. He was good to the community, the nicest human being you ever wanted to meet, but mean and vicious to his wife. He engaged in incredible physical violence. I always wondered why she just didn't leave, why she didn't take a piece of wood and just knock him in the head. But she stayed and took the abuse; apparently, she didn't have any place to go. And it broke my heart.

There has been so much violence against women in particular because our society is so male-oriented, and male-dominated. You know male chauvinism was at its worst during the early days of the civil rights movement.

I consider myself a pacifist and I detest violence. But at some point, you have to cross that line. In November 1992, right after the election, I took a congressional delegation to Somalia where I saw hundreds and thousands of people die. I saw little babies literally dying in their mother's arms. That's when I said we have to intervene. And that was the first time that I've said to our government, you've got to send troops, to save people, to keep people from killing other people.

Dworkin: I now think of myself as a failed pacifist, a lapsed pacifist. I see situation after situation where women are almost wrong not to use violence, not to stop the man in his tracks. He won't stop himself and the legal system won't stop him. Society leaves the woman isolated, to deal with his aggression, on her own, through whatever means she can manage.

Lewis: I don't have the answer, but I do think that sometimes we have to use radical non-violence. You have to be aggressive. Changes took place. One of my former colleagues said something that I thought was very derogatory about women, something that no one in a leadership position or no male in his right mind should ever say. He said that the position for women in the movement was a "prone position." Too many males in our society see women only in that light. That they're something to be used and abused. We have to change that mind set. We need something very radical. What's happening in American society is that we have almost become immune.

When you hurt another person, you are hurting yourself. It's a type of self-hatred. Because to deny someone else their own humanity, you're denying your own humanity. It's a lack of what

I call self-respect, self-worth; you've got to be superior. You've got to have power. You've got to control somebody. But we live in a community. We're not alone, we're family. I don't mean family in the traditional sense; I mean the human family.

We have to reveal a coalition that transcends sex, race, class, all of them. Because there are people in America that are being dehumanized. And we have to find a way to dramatize it so people can see it, people can feel it. They felt Selma. The American people couldn't stand seeing innocent people being trampled with horses and beaten with night sticks. And we have to find a way, even in Congress, even in the White House, the city halls, the state capitols, the board rooms, to sensitize, to make people feel it in their guts.

I think we have to organize and keep organizing. We don't rally anymore. We don't rock anymore. We don't march anymore. We don't stir up hell anymore. This country is too quiet, and the world is passing us by. We need to agitate.

Dworkin: I feel that the women's movement came directly out of the civil rights movement, sometimes in opposition to the male chauvinism of the civil rights movement, but also that it continues with the same goals that the civil rights movement had. Very inadequate sometimes, in being able to say what those goals are, with very impoverished means to confront society in a way that will make our meaning clear.

But I also find myself in a women's movement that refuses to do what is necessary. It wants to settle for the few gains for the few professional woman that made them. Still, the women's movement now is certainly an international movement. Yet in every country of the world, we see women who really think it's all right to have women on street corners selling themselves. They insist on defining that for us as an example of choice, instead of it being an example of what happens when you have been deprived of human sovereignty from the time you were a child. And that causes me great despair.

Lewis: Frederick Douglass said that in 1857: "There can be no progress without agitation." You've got to make some noise, you got to be willing to move. You cannot get lost. You cannot stay still. You have to have hope and you got to stay in motion. You cannot become bitter; you cannot become hostile. Women have got to continue to push. Life is a constant struggle. It shouldn't be. But it is a constant struggle.

You hang in there; you don't give up. You don't get lost in the sea of despair. You just keep going. And I tell you the journey that I've been on has been an incredible journey.

If someone had told me in 1963, when I was speaking at the March on Washington here when I was twenty-three years old or when I was being beaten on the bridge in Selma in 1965 when I was twenty-five, that one day I would be in Congress, in the leadership of the House, a Chief Deputy Majority Whip, that I would have an opportunity to go to South Africa and meet with Chief Buthelezi, Nelson Mandela, and then President Frederik de Klerk, and go back as an honored guest at their inaugural—I would have said you're crazy, you're out of your mind, you don't know what you're talking about.

So, I think that change is possible. You don't give up! And women must not give up! Just keep pushing. We have lost something in America. And maybe, maybe, just maybe, the rest of the world is going to teach us something. Because it was Arnold Toynbee who wrote: "It may be the Negro that takes a message of nonviolence to the Western world."

The world was mesmerized by what happened in South Africa. People by the hundreds, by the thousands, by the millions, wanted to vote in spite of the violence. They wanted to participate. We saw old women being pushed in a wheelbarrow to a polling place. We saw an old man coming on the back of his son to vote. We saw a person saying, "I voted. Now I can die. I can go home now."

What is radical nonviolence? I wondered. I had never thought about my work in those terms, but I had thought of it as radical *resistance.* I say to my staff all the time, "We are here. We're not going away. We will stand." In that way, I see Choices as an act of resistance. I view any clinic that opens now or remains open as an act of resistance. I'd like to see physicians resist by denying care until we can treat women according to their fundamental rights. I would consider this an act of radical nonviolence. In an article published in the journal *Social Medicine*, physician and author Martin Donohoe issued "a call for civil disobedience to my fellow physicians." He wrote:

> While Nazi comparisons are sometimes overused and not to minimize the horrors of the Holocaust, it remains noteworthy that unethical pronouncements regarding bodily integrity and patient care from a central authority is how Nazi medicine became an immoral agent of the state (similarly, Soviet psychiatry). History has shown us the value of widespread resistance to immoral laws (e.g., Dutch physicians during World War II, the U.S. Civil Rights Movement, the dismantling of Apartheid, the occupation of Lincoln Hospital by the Young Lords). Physicians have the right, indeed the obligation, to act when confronted with immoral laws that impact our patients' lives.[38]

Writing for *Truthout.org*, Donohoe continued:

> I have shared this idea on one of the major public health listservs and raised it with a number of colleagues at a major national public health meeting. The reluctance I have encountered from other medical workers indicates how much work has yet to be done to organize the medical sector and mobilize our community toward mass action. The initial responses I have received thus far have been minimal and muted; many said the idea was somewhat impractical, although upon further questioning admitted that they had not considered the idea and that they were concerned

---

38 Martin Donohoe, "A Proposal for Organized Civil Disobedience by Academic Medicine to the Supreme Court's *Dobbs v Jackson Women's Health Association* Decision," *Social Medicine*, Volume 16, Number 1, January–April 2023.

that a significant number of individuals may be afraid to join the civil disobedience. They favored slow change through elections, litigation, and public education campaigns. Nonetheless, failure to act in itself constitutes a negative action and weakens our profession's independence and moral standing.[39]

It appears that the medical establishment is either unaware of or in a state of denial about the "moral wound" that these draconian laws have now placed on physicians. It is imperative that health care workers, particularly physicians, do not become handmaids of the establishment but part of the vanguard of the resistance! Choices' assistant medical director Dr. Joseph Ottolenghi challenged a decision by the American Board of Obstetrics & Gynecology that will require OB-GYNs to take their certifying exams *in person in Texas*.

"It's hard to imagine a more dangerous place for abortion providers than Texas," Jessica Valenti pointed out in her newsletter *Abortion, Every Day*. "Doctors who perform abortions face up to life in prison, with civil penalties of at least $100,000. That's to say nothing of the physical risks: violence against providers and clinics has skyrocketed since *Roe* was overturned, with a 2022 study showing major increases in stalking, death threats, and invasions. . . . There's also something uniquely terrifying about the idea of hundreds of OB-GYNs, many of whom perform abortions, all descending on one publicly listed building at the same time in a state filled with anti-abortion sentiment, few gun regulations, and a recent spate of mass shootings. (ABOG's emailed promise that their staff is trained in "active shooter response" isn't all that reassuring.)"

I urge us to consider the *Dobbs* decision as the most organized codified legal example of *state violence against women*. And aside from all other legal, moral, religious, feminist, humanist, socialist, communist arguments against the overturning of *Roe*, we should

---

39 Martin Donohoe, "Doctors Have a Moral Obligation to Disobey Abortion Bans," *Truthout*, July 9, 2023, https://truthout.org/articles/doctors-have-a-moral-obligation -to-disobey-abortion-bans/.

consider expanding the Violence Against Women Act (VAWA) to the female population of this country—give them standing!

It is instructive to contrast Congressman Lewis's words with those of Susan Rosenberg, the activist and writer whom I interviewed in the late 1980s while she was in prison. In the 1970s and 1980s, Rosenberg had been active in the May 19th Communist Organization (M19CO), a far-left group that provided support to an offshoot of the Black Liberation Army, which had engaged in a number of armored truck robberies and bombings of government buildings.

Rosenberg had been living as a fugitive for two years while being sought in connection with the 1979 prison escape of Assata Shakur, a BLA member who had been convicted of murder, and the 1981 Brinks robbery when she was arrested in 1984 in possession of a large cache of explosives. She was given a fifty-eight-year prison sentence. What moved me toward Rosenberg and the reason I have done work with my Choices staff with women prisoners was an interest in how individuals accommodate paying the price for their actions.

I go back to my youth and fascination with Mary Queen of Scots and Elizabeth I. They have been juxtaposed as two sides of Janus—Mary the heart and Elizabeth the head, passion and reason, Dionysus and Apollo. Elizabeth the Virgin Queen, ultimate political strategist and brilliant tactician (never married), and Mary throwing her crown away for love (married three times, once to the murderer of her second husband). Later feminist analysis has moderated this black-and-white interpretation to a degree, but both paid a price for power.

And then there's Joan of Arc, also in prison—paying the price. Everybody that I was attracted to as a child, if they weren't killed, paid a heavy price. I was interested not only in the action and in the heroism, but in the payment of that price. I think of Madame Roland who upon facing the guillotine said, "Oh Liberty, what Crimes are committed in your name."

(An analogy can, of course, be drawn between being in a literal prison and being imprisoned by the state, as women are today.

Women had the ability to open those doors to freedom, during *Roe*. That door has closed.)

When I started to read about what was happening to Susan Rosenberg, I felt there were many points of connection between us. I didn't have the political experience that she did, but we came from Jewish intellectual backgrounds, and we made decisions based on our beliefs. I wanted to speak to her. I wanted to see the nature of how she thought about her actions, but also about the punishment, the price she had to pay for acting on those beliefs. In talking with her, what I found most inspiring was her ability to survive—her resilience. Carrying false identification at the time of her arrest, Rosenberg refused to reveal her true identity. The police had called in FBI agents, one of whom looked at her and told the police officer, "That bitch is a kike. Go check the records for a name."

"When I heard that," Rosenberg recalled, "I knew that I was at the beginning of a whole new stage of my life. I knew I had really been captured. Anti-Semitism in prison is really extreme, more so than I ever experienced growing up in New York. This has really pushed me along, along with my own internal processes, to fight very hard to be a Jew in prison." You never know how you will react when faced with a major moral challenge. You would like to think that you would be the person who would hide that Jewish family in your upstairs attic, risking your own and your family's. These are heavy prices. I wanted to speak to Rosenberg about the prices she paid.

> **Merle Hoffman:** If I were to say, "Who is Susan Rosenberg?" how would you define her?
>
> **Susan Rosenberg:** I would say I'm a revolutionary. I'm an anti-imperialist. I am a woman-oriented woman in the sense that I believe in and am totally committed to the liberation of women; and I'm a doctor of Chinese medicine and acupuncture.
>
> **MH:** Did you have any role models?
>
> **SR:** Emma Goldman. I read *Living My Life* when I was thirteen. I feel fortunate that I became part of a movement when I was in

my early teens. There was a sense that you could really change something. I guess I could say that I fell in love with the idea that people could control their own destinies, free of serious class, racial, and sexual differences. One of the most important things is an identification with the oppressed.

MH: Many people have feelings for the oppressed and the injustices of this world and many people connect on different levels of political struggle, but you put yourself at risk of completely losing your freedom. What motivated that level of activity?

SR: In part. I really believe that you have to do what you say you believe in.

MH: That includes armed struggle—does it not?

SR: I believed then and I believe now that, under international law, oppressed peoples/nations have the right to determine their own destinies, and that includes the right to wage an armed struggle—and that's happening all over the third world and it's happening here as well. I also believe that when you come from a country with the greatest war machine in the world and a country and a government that is responsible for state terrorism all over the globe, we, as citizens of this country, have an absolute responsibility to try and stop that. This was the most important way I could make a statement and say "No, this is not going to go on in my name as well." So, in that sense, I support armed struggle.

When you're in prison for a long time you get to think about and evaluate everything. I would look at the question of life and responsibility and armed struggle much more seriously now than ever before. But, I couldn't tell you that I would condemn violence.

MH: You know, there's a wonderful saying by Gandhi, "The means are an end in process." One must question what kind of "just society" is built on the foundation of armed struggle.

SR: I agree. It's something that I've thought a lot about in the last number of years. I wish I had then.

MH: So, in essence you are willing to stay in prison under intensely difficult conditions for the rest of your life?

SR: If I have to, that's what I'll do. It's not a pleasant thought but

I didn't do it for personal gain to begin with, and there wasn't anybody saying, "Do this." I think you have to take responsibility for your own actions.

MH: Do you see yourself as a martyr?

SR: No. I don't want to be.

MH: You may have to give up all hope for a so-called "normal life."

SR: Yes, but I like to think that the best part of my life is in front of me. I like to think, and I do think, that most of the contributions that I and the other imprisoned people in this case have to make are important. You have to make certain sacrifices.

MH: Are you a terrorist?

SR: No, I am not a terrorist—I've never been a terrorist. I'm against terrorism. I'm against terrorism on the right by the United States, and I'm against the terrorism on the left. Terrorism is a political and military strategy that I think is wrong.

MH: I think it's important to be said. The results of terror and violence have no politics. People can suffer from the activities of the right and/or the left.

SR: I'm against terrorism but I think the whole issue of violence, or a relationship to violence and terrorism, is complicated. There is violence in a system where you have 30 million people who have no health care—So, violence has many faces . . . I'm not involved in revolutionary social change because I love the violence—I think that violence has to be stopped. But I think that the most extreme and difficult forms of violence stem from the system under which we live.

MH: What is the essence of being a revolutionary?

SR: For revolutionaries there is the need to change the system fundamentally. I don't really think change can take place through politics without a complete restructuring of the system from beginning to end, from top to the bottom, but maybe it can. Maybe the kind of massive social upheaval that will take some resistance forms and legal forms will be able to do that.

MH: You are idealistic enough to still believe that people can change fundamentally?

SR: I hope so.

MH: Let's talk about women and feminism.

SR: I always felt independent and that being involved in social protest wasn't enough without a very clear and conscious struggle about women. I wouldn't say until recently I considered myself a feminist, although I was in on the Women's Liberation movement and involved in organizing and consciousness raising when I went to Barnard College.

MH: You saw class rather than gender as the primary oppression?

SR: It was both. Now I have much more of a commitment and dedication to the liberation of women. You know, being attacked as a woman in prison has been a really intense and ongoing experience—probably the worst part of being in prison. I was in Tucson before I was transferred to Lexington—we were sexually assaulted by federal prison guards. Males actually did the assault but the females who were in charge held us . . . it was a rectal and cavity search—a full body search. It was very intense . . . it took five women to hold me, and a man did the search. It's great, because whatever my actual immediate sexual orientation is now, I feel completely committed and dedicated to the full emancipation and human rights of gay and lesbian people. In our current society, homophobia dominates—I don't want to have any ideology that classifies, categorizes, oppresses or makes a judgment about what's an acceptable form of life and what isn't.

MH: So, in other words there can be no judgments about behavior?

SR: Oh no. There are societies that define a particular sexuality as being a type of decadent capitalism. I disagree with that. When you start quantifying oppressions, you're making a mistake. I also feel when you look at the world after you've been locked out for a long time, things become abstract.

MH: Let's say a revolutionary change takes place and a new order comes into being—your vision of a just social society, but people want to overthrow it because they find it intolerable to their moral value structure. If you were in a position of power, how would you deal with them?

SR: I don't think I'd put them in a prison. I don't believe in prisons anymore. I don't believe that prisons work.

MH: What do you do with felons and people who break the law?

SR: No state recognizes its own opposition or gives it legitimacy. I understand that completely; but there is an issue of being allowed to have human rights while being imprisoned. If there's going to be "special" treatment of us [harsher treatment, isolation] there should be recognition; there should be political prisons; we should be allowed to have political associations.

MH: They don't consider you political prisoners. They consider you terrorists. The judge compared you to drug dealers who shoot people on the street and then claim a political orientation.

SR: Well, I haven't shot anybody on the street . . .

MH: But they did pick you up with hundreds of pounds of guns and explosives.

SR: They did, but what I'm convicted of is possession, not use. We don't line people up against a wall and shoot them the way they do in every third world country. We kill them slowly over the years, bury them in prison, where the brutalization, the contempt and institutionalization is used as a means to destroy people's political commitments and beliefs.

MH: But then, it's very primitive psychology because if anything gives you more to live for, it's fighting for your beliefs, more opposition makes you stronger in your opposition. How do you deal with the rage and the frustration?

SR: I got sick at Lexington from that kind of rage. I didn't make myself sick, they made me sick. You get sick because you contain the rage.

I lost sleep. I wrote about it. I, too, feel that one day—consequences be damned . . . I'll fight for our dignity every time I can— what else can I do? There's really not much else to do. I get angry, I scream, I bounce off the walls—I hate men more and more and more every day. I don't mean it politically or quite that way, but it's increasingly difficult for me to navigate politely when the rage is contained—all of us are defined and labeled "terrorists"—and they're just waiting for us to riot . . . The issue is to never lose it. I never have in quite that way. That was the thing at Lexington. They pushed us and pushed and pushed . . .

MH: But they haven't broken you. You're still talking about the best years. That's a lot of energy positively directed.

SR: There's a poet I love a lot named Nazim Hikmet. He's a Turkish poet and a communist who brought epic poetry to that part of the world. He spent seventeen years in prison, and he got the whole thing when he talks about being captured and says that capture is not the point—the point is never to surrender. I think he's right—I agree with that as a mentality for living in what is basically a war between the government and us, so every time you survive, you win.

MH: Is there a message in all this?

SR: Dogma; you can't resist repression with dogma. As far as prison, the repressive apparatus tries to dehumanize you and create a mentality that's defined by brutality. If you abuse that humanity, then they win and you lose—you have to identify with the people that you're with and love them—understanding all the contradictions—there is something to be gained and learned from every inter-reaction at every level. It's a challenge to one's own continuing racism and arrogance. Even in this system where you get labeled to be the most extreme of the extremes, there's always a choice—at every corner.

MH: So, you would never see yourself as a victim?

SR: I've been victimized by the state in terms of its repressive apparatus; but, on a subjective level, no, I'm not a victim. I made my choices and commitments. I'll stand by that.

A revolutionary does not believe that whatever injustice they are fighting against can ever be changed from within the system. The system, therefore, must be overturned, and a new system built from the beginning. That is the essence of a revolutionary. I don't believe this. My thinking on human nature and my reading of history tells me that this never works out the way it is planned on paper.

I believe any system that people develop will have similar

problems to the system they replaced. Can people truly fundamentally change? Can any power rule innocently?

When I interviewed Chris Hedges, I asked whether it was possible to have power without evil, his answer was unflinching: "No. The question is not to get good people to rule—but how to keep people in power from doing evil. The problem with the Left is that it got seduced: it wants power. Social movements are necessary to keep power in check."

I will resist and resist and if my resistance turns into a revolution, then I will be challenged with a choice. After all, I am and always will be a radical. What became clear from talking to figures like John Lewis, Andrea Dworkin, and Susan Rosenberg was that revolution, resistance, reform—deeply divergent ways of looking at how to change a system—all require action. All require coming out of yourself and your own ego.

John Lewis followed Gandhi with a profound belief in passive resistance. Dworkin struggled to answer the question of whether that "tactic" could ever work for women and the battles they face, especially with their intimates and in their homes. Susan Rosenberg *acted* as a revolutionary but was seen and tried as a criminal. Still, she believed the cause trumped the state's definitions of what was right and what was just. We are all here for a very defined period of time. We must do what we see as right and necessary.

CHAPTER 8
LEADERSHIP AND POWER

The Politics of Power

Sophocles wrote that "nothing tests moral character better than the practice of authority and rule."

It was 1986 and I was sitting in Il Bocconcino on Sullivan Street in New York, having an Italian desert with my new friend, the feminist icon Phyllis Chesler. We were discussing the major rise in abortion clinic violence and how the response of the police was so tepid that it left staff feeling unsafe. Quoting Virginia Woolf, I told her that "women need a 'room of our own.'"

"No," Phyllis replied, "a country of one's own. A continent of one's own."

Then we discussed which one of us would be minister of defense or secretary of state. The dream then was that we could use some kind of legitimate state power to sweep in to rescue women in need. We would be a "feminist government in exile." Obviously, knowing the impossibility of the task, we started to focus on defensive power. Clinics were being attacked; the police were not making a difference. Why not take this on ourselves, with a community protective approach—like Curtis Sliwa and his Guardian Angels? We could have women patrolling the streets and subways, women escorting at abortion clinics. We discussed whether or not we would carry weapons and when we would use them.

In the end we decided to place ads in outlets like the *Village Voice* that read: "Women of New York City. Now is the Time, This is the Hour to Rise in Defense and Support of Women's Lives. The

Feminist Defense Brigade needs you. If you are mad as hell and can't take it anymore, volunteer for abortion clinic defense and civic neighborhood rape prevention patrol." It was a riff on the Uncle Sam-with-a-pointed-finger posters. We did not get a single response.

(Not to be deterred, I actualized the "Feminist Government in Exile" concept by creating a logo of an Amazon on horseback with her shield and sword, which I had made into T-shirts for Phyllis's fiftieth birthday party. Our dreams of power had morphed into product, but the vision remains.)

In 1995, I was in China for the World Conference on Women addressing an audience of Japanese feminist therapists and students. After my presentation, a young woman got up and asked a question. "As a feminist, how can you be comfortable using power in a therapeutic situation?" I responded that one has to define the nature of the power being referenced. So often when we speak of power it is as if power is a material thing in and of itself, as opposed to a dynamic state of interaction.

In politics, power is the capacity of an individual to influence the actions, beliefs, or behavior of others. There is personal power, which comes from personal characteristics, and positional power (authority), which comes from institutions. And this power can either be legitimate, or illegitimate and coercive. Leadership is the exercise of power. It depends on context, personality, geography, and history.

Recently there has been a tendency to define one's life trajectory as a "journey." If you consider a skilled therapist or counselor as someone who is further along that journey than you, then the sharing of wisdom of what obstacles may lie ahead is the kind of "power" that *should* be used. I am not speaking here of facts, but of wisdom, which is a very different thing. In the therapeutic situation which I was addressing (abortion counseling), I often called the counselors "facilitators."

Leadership and power were always issues within the feminist movement—Who should have it? Should anyone? There were calls in the early days for much of the feminist writing to be published anonymously, as if owning your own creation somehow went against the concept of "equality." But looking back at this now, perhaps it was an attempt to build a gorgeous metaphoric Gothic cathedral—in which no one who ever designed or worked on it had their name appear in any way. It was a collective prayer to God. But that degree of collectivity required a bit too much humility on everyone's part.

In the early days of the movement—the consciousness-raising days—there was a strong pull against any leadership. All of us had the power of our narratives, our "journeys," our lived lives. The personal was the political. Karl Marx said, "Men make their own history, but not as they please, in conditions of their own choosing, but rather under those directly encountered, given and inherited." It could be argued that women were not grounded in time and space—they had no history because they were not considered able to make any.

But in the women's movement of the twentieth century, recognition was critical. There was such a small place for any woman to shine, to gain attention for their work. So many feminists had minimal recognition for their work and press attention was a competition that was always shadowing the call for equity.

Leadership is not only press coverage. And I believe what also played into the vicious attacks against RiseUp had to do with the fact that we were covered extensively in the media. I do understand that so many women—and so many women in the movement—feel and felt their disappearance on the public stage, not only politically but personally. Being part of a movement can bring meaning. It allows openings for validation and reinforcement. In this age of the screen, if you are not visual and visualized, you do not exist.

Descartes's famous saying "I think therefore I am" could be translated into "I am in *The New York Times* therefore I exist." (Having been written up in 1978 by Francis X. Clines in the *New York Times* in a piece entitled "Love in a Very Small Space," I knew very well that particular sense of validation.)

But I have always been interested in the so-called great women and men of history—the decision-makers, the ones that acted on great stages. The ones whose decisions reverberated down through the centuries. This is why my fascination with Elizabeth I began as soon as I discovered her. Thinking back on this, this obsession may have occurred because I never really felt safe or in control of my environment when I was a child. I was also an only child, which meant I had all the love and attention of my parents—a blessing and a curse. I did not socialize much and had one or two very close friends, and as a result, I spent much of my time alone and learned how to be alone, but not lonely. Decisions were made on my behalf by individuals I felt instinctively were not on my "level." It was in my room where my imagination could run free—where I created a world where my will could be exercised.

I learned from my classical music education about the authority (power) of great teachers. I can see myself at sixteen with my music books going to my teacher Anka Landaus's home, practicing my Mozart sonata in my head so I would not make any errors when I played it for her. Entering her apartment was like entering a sacred place.

But it was not until many years later, after I had given up music and committed myself to my work at Choices, at the time of the first NAF conference, that I truly discovered my own sense of leadership. We had people from all over the country in attendance. They were speaking, debating, forming committees. I found that not only did I have a voice, but I had no problem expressing and articulating that voice. People responded to it—to me. I opened dialogues and fell very naturally into committee leadership and decision-making. I could work easily in coalitions.

One of the first things to know about learning how to lead is knowing how to follow. Aside from historical figures, Bella Abzug was really my only living inspiration and role model. When I worked as a volunteer with Bella, I was so excited to be in service to her, and to follow her lead. I learned very early on that people really need to feel involved; they need to feel that they are important, that their ideas are being validated. At Choices, I listen to everyone's opinions and then I tell them what my decision is. Ultimately, I'm the one responsible, so I have to be comfortable trusting my own decision-making. I call this a *collective autocracy*.

How do we keep our eyes on the prize, so to speak? How do

you speak to the pure vision to motivate and inspire? That is a challenge. Yes, you have to deal practically and operationally with the casualties of the war, in this case the women who cannot get access to legal safe abortion, who may die at the hands of the doctors who are afraid to save them. We have to continue fighting at the state level for them. But that does not mean we have to accept that fact and live with it forever.

The conversation on racial justice and the inclusion of Black women in leadership roles, for example, has taken on far more prominence and public presence since the overturning of *Roe v. Wade*, to the extent that there are calls for *only* women of color and women who have had abortions to become the leaders of the movement. While participation and leadership from women of color, Indigenous women, disabled women, nonbinary people, and so on, is critical (particularly because they are the ones who are most impacted by these egregious laws), we do not need identity leadership. We need people who have the skills, drive, and ability to lead, and we need mentors to assist them. It is also critical to move beyond identity politics and group egos to forge a truly united, comprehensive front against this assault by Christian fascists.

It is important to realize that there are not only group identities, but group egos. These egos were on full display against RiseUp when pro-choice groups actually challenged us by saying, "How dare you come into this fight, onto our turf?" These collective egos are open to the same political narcissism as those of the large nonprofits.[40] In my mind, how can you even begin to talk about turf? There should be no "turf" wars here. We have to fight the external enemies who are making women's bodies and lives *their turf!*

---

40 Indeed, in a recent research paper investigating "the relationship of left-wing authoritarianism with the ego-focused trait of narcissism" ("Understanding left-wing authoritarianism: Relations to the dark personality traits, altruism, and social justice commitment" by Ann Krispenz and Alex Bertrams in *Current Psychology*), the authors found that "some leftist political activists do not actually strive for social justice and equality but rather use political activism to endorse or exercise violence against others to satisfy their own ego-focused needs. We discuss these results in relation to the dark-ego-vehicle principle."

A Unified Message

Collaboration with other movements who were struggling for civil rights was a natural expression of our initial understanding that these struggles were in a sense a theme with variations. The theme was the recognition that there were social, institutional, and legal structures in this country that immobilize large groups of citizens, keeping them from fully participating in the equality vision of the Founding. Even clinics, who were usually competitive, put that competition into soft focus to come together to forge a strategy to defeat the invasions and harassment of Operation Rescue.

The "Members and Endorsers" page of my "Battle To Defend Abortion Clinics" pamphlet from 1988 illustrates the incredibly variety of support we had: Bella Abzug, ACT UP, Dr. Vickie Alexander, Charlotte Bunch, Phyllis Chesler, Center for Constitutional Rights, Hunter College, Third World Collective and Women's Studies, William Kunstler, New York University, Kate Millet, Asian Pacific American Law Students, NY Women Against Rape, NY Women in Criminal Justice, Organization of Asian Women, Oakland Feminist Women's Health, Princeton University, Revolutionary Communist Party, Dr. Helen Rodriguez Triaz, United Labor Action, and the Unitarian Church of Brooklyn.

There were early attempts to reach out to some leaders of the gay rights community, but aside from representatives of the Lavender Hill Mob at an early protest (a precursor of ACT UP), they never participated in any of our major actions or were a part of our strategic sessions. ACT UP, however, did take direct modelling and inspiration from our first pro-choice disobedience action at St. Patrick's Cathedral with their own action two months later.

But by and large, there was also no major gay or lesbian contingent that participated with our pro-choice coalition. So many lesbians were involved in the AIDS crisis and "supporting our brothers" that there seemed to be no time left for the sisters.

There was minimal if any participation on the part of the major civil rights or Black women's organizations. The abortion issues were somewhat contentious, and the community often followed the lead of the pastors who were not addressing this issue from their pulpits in any positive way. This was a great missed opportunity. It would have been tremendously helpful to have the Black religious leaders on board, because so many of the anti-abortion attacks always came cloaked in religious robes. I did work with and support one of the architects of the concept of "reproductive justice," Loretta Ross of Sister Song, who was always a colleague and someone whose work I respected.

We had the participation of Rabbi Balfour Brickner, who was with me at the "Back Alley Press Conference" (where I stated that if the assaults on legal abortion continue, "as I stand here in this filthy place I am standing in the future for thousands of American women"). But the main Jewish organizations were nowhere to be seen. Catholics for Free Choice was as involved as they could manage—but that was the extent of the support we had from the religious community. Currently, there is a more organized and public effort to support reproductive justice from the conservative and reform strands of Judaism, and I am currently working with Dr. Nori Rost, the clergy leader of the New York Society for Ethical Culture, to develop a strong supportive response to *Dobbs*.

Now, it is not that the movement is fractured, but that everyone is in lockstep. The movement *needs to allow debate and principled dialogue* because there are many people and many ideas within it. Again, here we should look to the civil rights movement, which was always in an open debate between leaders like Malcolm X and Martin Luther King Jr. There were questions of passive resistance vs. active resistance, questions of resistance vs. revolution, of radicalism and conservatism.

As the struggle changes, so must one's tactics and strategies. But the question to always keep in mind is: What is the goal? What is the goal of our movement now? How should this country—which is supposed to be a beacon of light, an example of equality and human rights, and where women make up more than half the population—respond to this crisis in women's health and freedom? What is the goal in this country where we must not be slaves to our biology and geography? It is asking a lot, but we cannot ask for anything less. Any unified message should include legal abortion nationwide. Abortion rights are paramount to women's freedom across the country and around the globe.

True political leadership is about more than supporting the appropriate policies and legislative agenda. It is ultimately about defining a broader social meaning within the context of communal values. Moral and visionary leadership should inspire people to be more than the least of their abilities. It should represent courage, loyalty, fortitude, authenticity, honesty, and intellectual integrity.

Where does feminism fit into all this? That depends. Feminism as a vision, as a radical way of defining and redefining the world, depends on judgments, often critical ones. Feminism as realpolitik— as practiced in everyday reality—often has to suspend those judgments. The ideologist asks the question: "Is it good for women?" The politician asks: "Is this the best we can do for women now?" The visionary holds to a higher standard, and takes the longer view.

Feminists may need to practice realpolitik to get the least bad candidate elected and the needed bills vetoed or passed, but feminism—even mainstream feminism—must continually articulate the transformative goals of the movement.

During the fifty years of *Roe*, there was an enormous increase in the number of women going into professional careers. Why? Because they had the ability to space out their children and make the decision about when and whether they would become mothers. Now that has been taken away and many women will be forced to have children when they don't want to. All of those gains that were made as a society are threatened.

I take no comfort in the fact that more women are increasingly finding themselves in positions of power. Counting the number of female CEOs is not the visionary goal of feminism. Here we are talking about careerism, and we are talking about the expectation that more women will be in more positions of power. And shall we count the women who have been in power but did not express anything near feminist goals? I can even pull my Elizabeth I off her pedestal by quoting her saying, "It is no marvel in a woman learning to speak, but there would be in teaching her to hold her tongue." But should the success of the feminist movement not be judged by the changes in the lived lives of all women?

The question remains: What is feminism and what is the feminist vision?

Was Barack Obama a feminist, as a *Ms. Magazine* cover that famously pictured him wearing a T-shirt with the words "This is what a feminist looks like" claimed? No; witness his tepid response to the killing of abortion provider Dr. George Tiller and his caving on support of abortion rights by denying abortion coverage in the health care bill provisions for women with preexisting conditions and not overturning Hyde.

"Funny," people would say to me, "you don't look Jewish."

"Funny, you don't look like a concert pianist."

"Funny—you don't look like a feminist."

But I was all of those things and more. And equally today, as we struggle to define a new standard of feminism, appearance, age, dress, sexual orientation, gender orientation, and labels are merely detours, diversions, and performance. Thought and action are the fault lines that matter.

The Feminist Litmus Test

So, what is a feminist?

To be clear, I would be quite comfortable without the feminist label.[41] At this point in my life, I do not use any pronouns. Rather,

---

41 There are many brands of feminism. New feminism is a form of feminism that emphasizes the integral complementarity of women and men, rather than the superiority of men over women or women over men, and advocates for respecting persons from conception to natural death. Intersectional feminism is "a prism for seeing the way in which various forms of inequality often operate together and exacerbate each other," according to Kimberly Crenshaw, an American law professor who coined the term in 1989. In an interview with *Time* Crenshaw explained, "All inequality is not created equal. We tend to talk about race inequality as separate from inequality based on gender, class, sexuality, or immigrant status. What's often missing is how some people are subject to all of these, and the experience is not just the sum of its parts."

I identify as a "second-class citizen." In the words of Rebecca West, "People call me a feminist whenever I express statements that distinguish me from a doormat." I am a heterodox thinker and take wisdom anywhere I find it.

At its root, feminism calls for the understanding, validation, and acceptance of women as human, having within them what has historically and scientifically been seen as the thing that separates us from the rest of the animals: our ability to reason. Reason is defined as the mental powers concerned with forming conclusions, judgments, or inferences. And reason is the faculty that is used to determine whether to bring a pregnancy to term.

Anyone who would work politically to place women and girls in a position where they are banned from using their own reason to determine when and whether to be a mother—and to subsume their moral reasoning to that of mainly male elected officials, resulting in forcing women to bear unwanted children—supports slavery. Again, it is a question of who the chooser is. Regardless of groups like Feminists for Life, any woman who does not support abortion rights cannot be a feminist. Period.

There are many individuals who need to reclassify themselves from anti- to pro-choice. These are the people who say, "I would never have an abortion, but that is my choice, and I would not stop any other woman from doing so." These individuals must be differentiated from those who feel and think that they would never ever have an abortion and no woman should. Those are the people who will work politically to attain that goal. Those who would work to ensure that *all* women and girls do not have access to legal safe abortion are those who must be fought and defeated. These people should never use the term "feminist."

The fundamental right to reproductive freedom and justice stems from the recognition of the fundamental humanity of women in any society, exercised in their ability to reason and choose. The ultimate choice, of course, involves control (power) over their reproduction—the ultimate "means of production" in Marxist terms. By ceding this power to the state or church, women lose their humanity to the hypothetical humanity of either the fetus or to the "collective good" as those in power define it. Feminism should not be about gender, age, race, or class. It is about the vision of equality and justice for over half of humanity. And the line in the sand is reproductive justice.

Picture all the women and young girls and people of conscience fighting for reproductive justice in whatever way they are able: in their college classrooms and in their workplaces, at their computers and on iPads, or out in the world. Embrace them. But always challenge their thinking, because they are not what they wear, who they fuck, or what they buy. They are what they think, and what they do about what they think. In the words of Barbara Strickland, "What I am proud of, what seems so simply clear, is that feminism is a way to fight for justice, always in short supply."

Revolution Lite

Oscar Wilde, writing in *The Soul of Man Under Socialism*, said, "A map of the world that does not include Utopia is not worth glancing at, for it leaves out the one country at which Humanity is always landing." Unsurprisingly, women have been assigned supporting roles in even the most expansive male-imagined Utopias. Yet, modern-day feminists seem to have lost the art of visionary mapmaking altogether.

The first voyager to Utopia was Plato, who in *The Republic* created a society that utilized the energies of all people. Women's reproduction did not keep them from playing a citizenship role (children were to be raised communally). Plato insisted that women were capable of the same tasks as men, although he assumed they would be inferior in performing them.

Thomas Moore, writing centuries later in *Utopia*, took the Platonic position of utilizing all citizens' skills for the good of society. His vision was less progressive than Plato's, but women were fully functioning members of society. Women farmed, learned trades, fought battles along with their husbands, and were educated—a radical concept in sixteenth-century England.

While women fared well enough in these imaginative landscapes of male Utopias, their real-time lives continued to be subservient and powerless. War, poverty, violence, early death, discrimination, and terror continued to create the contours of their existence. When visionaries did manage to "land on Utopia," it was usually a crash landing with multiple casualties. The first major landing was the French Revolutionaries, who, in attempting to create a new world with "reason" as their God, left a landscape of headless corpses. The American Revolution, taking much of its philosophy from the French Enlightenment, made "life, liberty, and the pursuit of happiness" the triad of its Utopian vision. Unfortunately, in Jefferson's "workshop of liberty," women and enslaved Black people were completely left out.

In *Thinkers of the New Left*, Roger Scruton sees the two goals of liberation and social justice as not obviously compatible, any more than the liberty and equality advocated in the French Revolution. He asks an important question—"If liberation involves the liberation of individual potential, how do we stop the ambitious, the energetic, the intelligent, the good-looking, and the strong from getting ahead, and what should we allow ourselves by way of constraining them?"

Some early visionaries of the "feminist revolution" of the twentieth century had a concept of a gender-neutral egalitarian society where women would be able to "be all they could be." Indeed, the rhetoric of the movement often stressed that a successful landing on this Utopia would be soft and benefit not only women, but also men and male institutions. Men would learn or be taught to welcome a radical change in their personal and political power positions.

The vision outlined in Betty Freidan's 1963 book, *The Feminine Mystique*, said to have sparked the "second wave" of feminism, was one of freedom from the "problem that had no name." She saw the freedom to become a fully engaged person as the "personal" and the goal of a gender-neutral society that would have no barriers to women's self-fulfillment as the "political."

Unlike the civil rights struggles of the twentieth century that were triggered by attacks and assaults against African Americans, leaving a sordid trail of bloodshed, the feminist revolution did not emerge from widespread physical violence, although terror and poverty crushed many women's lives. Women's biological and historical inheritance of murder—through wars, rapes, domestic violence, botched childbirth, and illegal abortions—remains a continual, though unanswered, scream for radical action.

Now, after so many years, we still struggle to express a collective definition of what feminism is or is not. If one can't even name the boundaries or contours of the vision, or agree on what a feminist is, then we are left with feminism as a meme or a product. Indeed, the greatest casualty of the feminist revolution may be the feminist vision itself. In a society where everything from sex to war and revolution is commodified, branded, and packaged to sell, feminism can become another box on the shelf. One only has to witness what is defined as "empowering." A recent piece in the *New York Times* entitled "Who Gets to Wear G-Strings Now?" quotes one college counselor as saying, "Wearing a G-string is 'liberating,' because it symbolizes 'taking ownership of your body.'"[42]

A Kiss Is Just a Kiss

I am no naïf. I know that politics is the art of compromise, and that, as one major liberal New York political operative told me long ago, "There are no issues, only elections." I think back to 1985—not an unusually dangerous year. There was a rash of fire bombings at abortion clinics; a physician had been kidnapped; and my secretary was attending a course with the Bureau of Alcohol, Tobacco, and Firearms to teach her how to correctly open my mail so that she could avoid being blown away by a letter bomb. It was, after all, business as usual for those of us on the front lines of the abortion wars.

Meanwhile, on the political front, the Reagan administration asked the Supreme Court to overturn *Roe v. Wade* and return the

---

42 Mya Guarnieri, "Who Gets to Wear G-Strings Now?" *The New York Times*, July 16, 2023, https://www.nytimes.com/2023/07/16/style/g-string-thong-trend.html.

right to regulate abortion to the states. At the same time, high on the anti-choice agenda was a human life amendment that would make the fetus a "constitutional" person and violent clinic invasions led by Operation Rescue. In response, I formed the New York Pro-Choice Coalition and was organizing a rally and march to celebrate *Roe*. It was a time of meetings and politics during which I met Senator Bob Packwood.

Packwood was an early and ardent player in the abortion struggle, a staunch and able ally of the pro-choice forces on the Republican side of the Senate. After meeting him at a New York fundraiser for abortion rights and soliciting and receiving a piece from him for what was then the fifth issue of the *On the Issues* newsletter, he called to request a meeting at a New York City hotel. Unaware of any rumors of any "loutish" behavior on Packwood's part, I approached our meeting with a mixture of curiosity and anticipation.

Our conversation ranged from the political to the philosophical to the personal. We discussed the existential nature of power and what causes we would die for. He seemed to be genuinely moved by the responsibilities of his position. During the conversation, he complimented me on my dress, my style, my intelligence, and the energy of our interaction. The exalted nature of his position did not influence my feelings toward him. I did not find myself physically attracted to him, and because I showed no interest, I did not expect the embrace and attempted French kiss in the middle of Park Avenue as I hailed a cab.

On reflection, this story has little importance in either my political, psychological, or personal history. The first question I asked myself was whether or not I shared any of the reactions described by the women who have come forward to accuse him of sexual harassment. I am of course aware of the difference in my position regarding Packwood. I did not volunteer or work for him. Unlike Gena Hutton, Packwood's 1980 campaign chairwoman who described her first reaction to his advances as one of "shame," believing that since "he was the great person I thought he was . . . this had not happened with other people," I felt no shame or amazement. I was not prone to assume that men who did good deeds in the public arena were necessarily good boys in the private realm. Packwood's sexual come-on was just that. The fact that it was more an adolescent groping than a sophisticated seduction was more of an annoyance than a threat. I still thought highly of our conversation. I enjoyed the fact that we had connected, and I found that I still respected Packwood the senator in the morning.

Packwood the man is a different story. A piece in the *New York Times* described the fire against him by women's groups as being fueled by a sense of "betrayal." Was Packwood's early support of abortion rights, it asked, a true expression of avant-garde Republican liberalism or a form of political opportunism?

Paige Wagers was a twenty-one-year-old awestruck mail clerk in Packwood's office in 1975 when Packwood pulled her hair back and stuck his tongue into her mouth. Uncomfortable, she eventually left the job for another government position. Six years later she met him on Capitol Hill, and as they walked through a basement corridor, he pulled her into an empty office toward a couch. She repulsed him, and Packwood let her go, but the memories remain painful.

"He totally sucked me in because of all the flattering things he said to make me trust him. So that moment, I died inside. I was humiliated. I wasn't even human to him. I was like a dog, someone who couldn't possibly have feelings."

According to Patricia Ireland, president of National Organization of Women (NOW), "It's an insult to the Senate that he or anybody else would not have known it was wrong to tear at a woman's clothing, to stand on her toes, to stick his tongue in her mouth."

An affront, yes; an annoyance, yes; an insult, yes. But the women who came forward to accuse Packwood spoke of feeling intimidated and threatened, and in a way that seemed to scar them for life. By all accounts his pathetic sexual overtures were immediately withdrawn when he was rejected, and of course the women felt violated and enraged, as well they should. But why did they feel permanently devastated? How could he hold such powerful emotional sway? Did Packwood's fall from grace seem all the more egregious to his accusers because of his position? Were they disappointed that his power was not pure, that a senator who fought politically for women's rights was perhaps a pathetic regressed adolescent? How is it that any man could make us feel like a dog—something less than human—just by attempting a boorish pass?

What about Bill Clinton? I did not hear any feminist calling his behavior with Monica Lewinsky an "insult" to the presidency. Quite the opposite. In "Feminists and the Clinton Question," a masterful display of realpolitik feminism published in *The New York Times*, Gloria Steinem wrote that if all the sexual allegations against Clinton were true, then he might be "a candidate for sex addiction." She also cited polls that showed many Americans believed Clinton was lying, but that there was sympathy for keeping "private behavior private." In essence, Clinton was given a pass because of his politics.

More recent examples abound: New York Attorney General Eric Schneiderman—the attorney general who brought the case against the Antis in front of Choices, a major opponent of President Donald Trump, and a vocal supporter of abortion rights—positioned himself as a combatant of sexual harassment and abuse at the height of the #MeToo era. When *The New Yorker* won its Pulitzer for coverage of sexual harassment, Schneiderman issued a congratulatory tweet, praising "the brave women and men who spoke up about the sexual harassment they had endured at the hands of powerful men." Then, in the spring of 2018, four women accused him of physical violence and abusive, demeaning behavior. Schneiderman denied the accusations but resigned within hours. The hypocrisy of such men has unfortunately ceased to amaze me!

In her latest book, *Penile Imperialism: The Male Sex Right and Female Subordination*, Sheila Jeffreys argues that the founding principle of this imperialism is the "male sex right"—the assertion that men are, by birthright, entitled to access and use the bodies of women in pursuit of sexual gratification. Since female bodies exist to be used by men, there are no "wrong" ways to use them.

Whatever damage men do to women while exercising their sex right is really of secondary importance at best. Her rights, her privacy, her freedom, her ability to participate in society, even her survival, are irrelevant. While this principle operates in terms of prostitution and intimate partner violence, it is writ large in what the *Dobbs* decision has done to women—turning them into breeders for the state and slaves to their geography and biology.

What and who diminishes us? We are all diminished now by what the Supreme Court has done—we are all second-class citizens. Does it get any lower than that? Why do we have to do the psychological work of the oppressors for them? How can we allow anyone—any man—to kill us "inside," in that place where no one should be allowed without invitation.

We must develop an inner sense of value, confidence, and self-worth despite all the sociopolitical messages to the contrary. If every unwanted look, stupid remark, and sexual gesture has the power to make us feel "less than human," then what kind of power can women ever lay claim to? What revolution is this whose participants can be laid siege to with a look or vanquished with a kiss?

Happiness and the Feminist Mind

The findings of the latest Gallup poll on happiness are telling. According to CNN, "in 2020, before the pandemic began, an average of 48 percent of Americans said they were satisfied. There was a big drop in 2021, when 41 percent indicated they were happy with what was going on these twenty-nine different metrics." When it came to questions of policy, "35 percent are satisfied on the sixteen areas measured consistently over the last two decades. Some of these policy issues include the nation's abortion policies, the policies to reduce crime, the state of the economy and the quality of education in our nation. This 35 percent is the lowest ever measured."[43]

---

43 Harry Enten, "American Happiness Hits Record Lows," CNN, February 2, 2022, https://www.cnn.com/2022/02/02/politics/unhappiness-americans-gallup-analysis/index.html.

Americans are a nation of people who feel supremely entitled to happiness. After all, in the first paragraph of the Declaration of Independence, Thomas Jefferson virtually orders us to pursue it. Calling the Declaration "an expression of the American mind," Jefferson proclaimed for future generations that the pursuit of happiness, along with life and liberty, were inalienable rights.

What is happiness? The dictionary defines it as the result of chance, something impersonally positive that befalls one like good luck. Pioneering French philosopher Blaise Pascal believed that because of its arbitrary nature, "we never live, but we hope to live and as we are always preparing to be happy, it is inevitable we should never be so." And Michel de Montaigne, French Renaissance humanist, even more pessimistically stated that "no man should be called happy until after his death, for human affairs are uncertain and variable and the slightest shock may change them from one state to another wholly different."

How did happiness, an essentially ephemeral, affective personal state, become defined as an objective and obtainable object of pursuit? The philosophical roots of the Declaration were in Aristotle, who had definite theories on the meaning and nature of happiness. He saw it as a virtuous activity that resulted from education, the pursuit of wisdom, and participation in community affairs.

Our country's framers had a realistic view of human nature. They recognized the existence of self-interest but did not view it as an end in itself. Today, more than two hundred years after the drafting of the Declaration of Independence, happiness has been depoliticized. Happiness has become property, something that can indeed be pursued and captured.

It is this tension between personal happiness and transcendent political good that continues to challenge feminists. How do we navigate between the two? What language do we use? What concepts? Women have also pursued happiness, but with a difference. In a variation of the Jeffersonian ideal of the pursuit of happiness leading to the responsibilities of citizenship, women were educated and conditioned to believe that their ultimate happiness lay in serving others, ideally through marriage and through the birthing and rearing of children. However, it was not enough for women merely to pursue and achieve this kind of happiness; it was also their full responsibility to maintain it for the entire family, ideally through self-sacrifice.

For women, the American state that Madison called the "workshop of liberty" became the family. As a result, women far more than men have viewed happiness (defined as a successful relationship) as the measure by which they would judge their lives.

The feminist movement profoundly challenged this assumption of derivative happiness. It also profoundly challenged the assumptions of social and political reality. Traditional political theory taught that there was an ironclad distinction between the private (personal) and the public (political). The radical genius of the movement's prime insight upended that idea and the feminist mantra was born: The personal is political.

According to early theorists, the separation of the personal and public spheres was not inherent in the nature of things; it was a social construction. As a result, women began to see and to teach others that the narratives they developed to name and construct their lives were not merely expressions of individual journeys, but were reflections of centuries of traditions and institutionalized sexism, which is what is generally called "patriarchy." The stories we women tell ourselves and each other about why our lives are far from what we expected are just that—stories.

It is not because you are not intelligent enough, or ambitious enough, or don't work hard enough, but because you are a woman in a society that does not value you—particularly if you are not white. Women's personal realities and much of their physical and psychological sufferings reflected their second-class citizenship and their oppression under patriarchy rather than any inherent gender truth.

Simone De Beauvoir famously wrote that "one is not born, but rather becomes, a woman." Feminism taught that a woman's life—her "feminine" essence—was essentially political. Sex, gender, reproduction, economics, age, beauty, romance, sexual orientation—all were up for grabs to be deconstructed, analyzed, and redefined through the feminist lens. Only happiness did not receive the benefits of deconstructive analysis and remained apolitically in the realm of the personal.

In search of a definition, happiness cloaked itself as having it all or as the pursuit of sexual pleasure without the constraints of "penile imperialism." The idea of choice itself (rather than what was chosen) and the primacy of orgasm by any means necessary became litmus tests for what was considered by many to be feminist. Of course, this was opposed by "radical feminists"; anti-pornography, anti-prostitution (sex work), and anti-surrogacy feminists; among others. "I am a feminist," said Andrea Dworkin. "Not the fun kind."

Perhaps one of the most common expressions of the personal becoming an unrealistic, demanding political is the desire and expectation to "have it all." I have listened to many women recount their deep disappointment with the feminist revolution because fifteen or twenty years later they do not have a brilliant career, a loving lover or family, enough money for financial security, a great publisher, or a high quotient of self-esteem. In fact, so many of the brilliant early voices and visionaries ended their lives in poverty and despair. Many felt the movement failed them, it didn't deliver. That was what the revolution was about, wasn't it—giving women the opportunity to do their own thing, to do what makes them happy? Emma Goldman's famous quote, "*If I can't dance, I won't be part of your revolution,*" expresses what became a deep theme among many feminists. It insinuates that the movement owes women ongoing happiness.

For women, and especially for political activists or feminists working to radically change the world, pursuing personal happiness through the movement can be a dangerous detour. It translates into the expectation that life, the movement, the revolution owes you. The movement owes us nothing—which is not to say that one cannot experience great joy in radical action.

Pursuing personal happiness can lead us to expect loyalty and friendship from political comrades when we should work for functional and strategic alliances. In fact, one should not expect true loyalty or connection from people you do politics with. Such expectations, when disappointed, can lead us to leave political work when we are burned out and despairing because we've been doing this ten, twenty, thirty, fifty years, and the world hasn't changed fast enough. It can make us feel we've failed if we do not achieve political goals that decrease our personal alienation or misery. And it can lead to feminists' turning on the movement and one another in fury and recrimination because the promise of a brave new world hasn't changed theirs enough.

Revolutions are not undertaken for fun. Which is not to say that one cannot or should not have some or even a great deal of fun while in them. The idea that the continuing feminist revolution was and is about making individual women happy and fulfilled is a continuing error. If some feminists involved in the movement were personally unhappy but the movement achieved even some of its goals of freeing women from violence, oppression, and the tragedies of half-lived lives, it would be a success.

If we ever "dance at the revolution," it is because we are listening to a different drummer, the one that sounds the notes of commitment to a cause and the music of the transcendence that comes from working for the highest ideals.

If feminism is to count for anything beyond a mere interest group, we must vigilantly guard its vision. We cannot bend it to compromise or change direction in response to popularity polls. Our standards should be raised even higher for those in public life who would carry our banner or espouse our principles.

All rights start with the body. We are embodied creatures—and women far more than men because our reproductive abilities are the source, the core, the prime objective of society's control and oppression of us.

Theory must become practice at one point in time. Our bodies are where the power structures make their marks with their laws, religions, traditions, and prejudices. Our bodies are lines in the sand. Each one of us proclaims that the power of the state stops at our skin when we lay our bodies down for an abortion, saying, with that action, that it is we who will decide when and whether to bear children. Or when we leave a violent relationship. Or when we resist and when we take the right to sexual pleasure. And when we declare that we must live in freedom. When you draw a line in the sand, you have to be prepared to defend it, to take risks and embrace challenges. That, too, calls upon the body, as well as the body politic.

The message of the Supreme Court decision has not only been that women are second-class citizens, but that the contributions of women in all fields of public life are superfluous. As science continues to "progress" at a speed that both challenges our understanding and upends traditional power structures, and reproductive technology exceeds the bounds of imagination, feminism itself may need a new ideology. We may need a non-aligned religion or organized secular institution to debate and come to some collective understanding of what to do with the enormous power we hold. John Lewis speaks of his "beloved community" of shared values. We have to ensure that feminism speaks to equality, compassion, education, and justice. And we have to answer the challenge of navigating the tension between individual achievement and the forces needed to control it.

We must consider, for example, the rise of artificial intelligence and how it will recast humans themselves. On May 1, 2023, *The New York Times* reported that more than one thousand technology leaders and researchers signed an open letter warning that AI technologies present "profound risks to society and humanity."

"Because these systems deliver information with what seems like complete confidence, it can be a struggle to separate truth from fiction when using them. Experts are concerned that people will rely on these systems for medical advice, emotional support, and the raw information they use to make decisions."

Will there still be "genders" in fifty or one hundred years? With the ability to create bodies and minds through AI, will the fluidity of "gender" have a set point? Will we be living in a simulation of the "real" world? A complete "Truman Show"? Will we conquer death at last? Should we? Where should feminism stand be on these issues? Wherever we stand, we must have a seat at the table when these profound discussions take place.

CHAPTER 9
PASSING THE TORCH

The Challenge of Inspiring Young People

The Australian feminist Dale Spender once wrote, "When I learnt, however, that in 1911 there had been twenty-one regular feminist periodicals in Britain, that there was a feminist book shop, a woman's press, and a woman's bank run by and for women, I could no longer accept that the reason I knew almost nothing about women of the past was because there were so few of them, and they had done so little."

Reading this, I think about my young self in the library on Jamaica Avenue discovering Elizabeth I and thinking she was the only woman in the world with power. A warrior queen who ruled alone. What, I wondered, were the roads not taken if I had the knowledge of those other women throughout history to inspire and guide me?

There is this old Creole saying: "Tell me who or what you love, and I can tell you who you are." We have become a population where we are what we see in an ongoing feedback loop. The rise of "influencers" who can speak for a brand and the narcissism of personal self-representation has reached a point of self-parody. Everything everywhere pushes, moves, directs us to an external self-definition. We are determined by the number of likes on our posts. Whatever space we have for interiority and critical thinking becomes a barren field for the meme of the day.

Most celebrities are not role models. They are products. The causes that they support, the clothes that they wear, and the stands that they take are very carefully curated to ensure that their brand remains strong (and profitable). Some of our role models of women in corporate and political power are finding out that they should be careful of what they wish and work for. The year 2023 has witnessed the resignations of three women in leading positions: the prime minister of New Zealand, Jacinda Ardern; the leader of the Scottish Independence Party, Nicola Sturgeon; and Susan Wojcicki, CEO of YouTube and a founding member of Google.

The two political leaders said that their decisions were motivated by feeling that they were no longer able to give their best to their countries. Wojcicki said that she wants to dedicate herself to her family, her health, and personal projects which inspire her passion. The 2022 Women in the Workplace survey stated categorically that "We're in the midst of a 'Great Breakup.'" Key findings from the study[44] included the facts that:

Only 1 in 4 C-suite leaders is a woman, and only 1 in 20 is a woman of color.

The "broken rung" is still holding women back: For every 100 men promoted from entry level to manager, only 87 women are promoted, and only 82 women of color are promoted.

Now, women leaders are leaving their companies at higher rates than ever before. To put the scale of the problem in perspective: for every woman at the director level who gets promoted, two women directors are choosing to leave their company.

The reasons women leaders are stepping away from their companies are telling. Women leaders are just as ambitious as men, but they're more likely to experience belittling microaggressions, such as having their judgment questioned or being mistaken for someone more junior. They're doing more to support employee well-being but this critical work is spreading them thin and going mostly unrewarded. And finally, it's increasingly

---

44 Alexis Krivkovich, Wei Wei Liu, Hilary Nguyen, Ishanaa Rambachan, Nicole Robinson, Monne Williams, Lareina Yee, "Women in the Workplace 2022," *McKinsey*, October 18, 2022, https://www.mckinsey.com/featured-insights/diversity-and -inclusion/women-in-the-workplace.

important to women leaders that they work for companies that prioritize flexibility, employee well-being, and diversity, equity, and inclusion. If companies don't take action, they won't just lose their women leaders; they risk losing the next generation of women leaders, too.

The microaggression of mistaking a manager for someone more junior will be remembered fondly, along with the macro-aggression of the *Dobbs* decision currently placing twenty-three million women in a position of having absolutely no access to legal abortion. These corporations have already lost the "next generation of women leaders" in all the states that have made legal abortion all but impossible. Social attitudes rarely change as quickly as the law—which is why Ruth Bader Ginsburg believed that *Roe* was not the most optimal vehicle for the legalization of abortion.

Yes, women may have definitely been discouraged if their companies did not prioritize diversity, equity, and inclusion. Now they not only should be discouraged but enraged and activated that their country has placed them in a position of second-class citizenship. In *The Feminist Industrial Complex*, Charlotte Alter argues that "simply placing women in high-ranking jobs is not enough. Social attitudes matter. If these prominent women are treated with social disdain—if derision and hostility lower their status, despite their title—following in their footsteps becomes unappetizing. Women are actively deterred from the job. The idea that 'role models' are central to female aspiration is patronizing."

"Patriarchy," she writes, "is a system of rewards and deterrents, in which the punishment of overachieving women is just as important as the praise of submissive ones. Which is to say that handing a woman a poisoned chalice of a job is not quite the feminist victory some might think it is."

I would agree that patriarchy is a system of rewards and punishments; whether the punishment becomes a deterrent is up to the actor—the individual woman. If she believes that this diminishment is "unsurvivable" then of course it is a deterrent. But if we truly understand that true social change takes decades and generations, then we must view this as the price to be paid for being a pioneer.

I have often quoted Olive Schreiner who in 1911 wrote an excellent description of the price of being first in *Woman and Labour*: "It is the swimmer who first leaps into the frozen stream who is cut sharpest by the ice; those who follow him find it broken, and the last find it gone. It is the men or women who first tread down the path which the bulk of humanity will ultimately follow, who must find themselves at last in solitudes where the silence is deadly." I would agree that no one woman with a bit of gumption can overcome centuries of entrenched misogyny, which is why I have always argued that this struggle for women's freedom is a generational one—but I would disagree that a hit in social status is unsurvivable.

It is an old political idiom that "morality cannot be legislated." Even though there have been observable gains in terms of laws and social policy that express feminist concepts, they are not actualized into the realities of most women's everyday lives. We need to learn resilience, patience, and what price there is to pay for ambition and breaking away from the herd. Who are the role models for that? We must first motivate young people to understand the value of taking risks, of pushing beyond the mere performative aspects of political engagement to the real work of resistance.

RiseUp did what no other movement on this issue has done since *Dobbs*: they have gained the engagement of thousands and thousands of high school and college students. Most of these youth were political virgins, and I am so proud that they came to experience through our work. Whether or not their political engagement continues remains to be seen. But there is individual responsibility here. We can inspire, catalyze, mentor, teach, and preach—but we cannot do the work for them! Responsibility for action remains an individual choice!

It is crucial to understand that being an activist will never mean one march or one action. A long-term commitment is required. No great social movement ever progressed without a rising of individuals—individuals who create another kind of identity through their masses and their demand for justice. Some have wondered publicly if the time for collective action has ended. I still believe that the rage needs expression. Marches, rallies, and demonstrations are not only productive outlets for anger but can in and of themselves change the political reality of those in power.

Attention must be paid. Legal and social change takes time, sometimes a very long time. Changes of the heart require unity, patience, sustained attention, and an understanding of the role that you are playing. With an impending recession and the collective mental health crisis coming out of the COVID-19 pandemic, is it any wonder that so many of us would like to stay in bed literally and figuratively and pull a blanket over ourselves?

We need to revisit our philosophies—is it time for a change of definition, of vision, of values? A different definition of virtue? Since the 1960s, there has been a move away from enlightenment meritocracy back toward group identity as the grounding and definition of individual identity. This has come mainly from the left and the feminist movement. We speak as if the boundaries of nature/nurture themselves have become so fluid that the definitions are open to individual interpretation. We may have become like those in Plato's cave, who think we are looking at reality, when we are really looking at shadows.

It seems obvious that what gets defined as feminist values now aligns very closely with "woke" values—that is group (particularly gender) identity, acceptance of intersectionality, and a heightened vigilance concerning triggers and safe spaces in the service of equity of results, as opposed to equality of opportunity. Amid all the performances and virtue signaling, what is the definition of virtue for feminists? We need to go back to basics and question what actions, behaviors, and beliefs we consider feminist.

Google "feminist values" and you will find different iterations of the following idea:

> Feminism is a range of sociopolitical movements and ideologies that aim to define and establish the political, economic, personal, and social equality of the sexes. Feminism holds the position that

societies prioritize the male point of view and that women are treated unjustly in these societies.

A Lesson in Criticism

Once, as a young music student, I performed in an annual master class. This was a great honor because only the "best" students were invited to play for the "master." The audience was filled with proud parents, other teachers, friends, grandparents. The students would get up and perform something they had practiced, while the "master" would sit in the back shouting "*andante*," "*allegro*," or "play that phrase again."

I was twelve or thirteen years old, and very nervous. My mouth was dry, and my hands were visibly shaking. I remember playing Chopin's waltz in C-sharp minor. As soon as I started, he began ripping into me. Every three bars he would shout something I had to change or repeat.

I managed to get through it and walked off the stage to my teacher who was waiting outside the auditorium. She was about eighty years old then, with silver hair tied tightly in a bun. I was hysterical with shame and embarrassment. "You were wonderful. It was great," she said. "He only criticizes people he thinks have talent. He wouldn't waste his time otherwise."

This was a profound lesson. For the first time, I was challenged to regard criticism as a positive. My teacher taught me that a serious critique is not an attack but a catalyst toward excellence.

One must be so careful now. I get a huge amount of blowback. I have to navigate different levels of relationships with great care. With my employees at Choices, I have to listen to things I absolutely disagree with and often not say anything. If I do reply, the response is usually extensively edited.

I have seen this mentality become codified in recent years. Everyone considers themselves to be under attack. There is no separation between people and ideas, which fosters an extremely limiting environment. So, one must be open to criticism. I have changed some of my behavior through a lot of feedback from staff at Choices, particularly how I communicate.

Chris Hedges, whom I interviewed about the nature of the current American reality, considers it death-focused and said that the only thing that could save us was love. Love was a code word for compassion. He defined love as "the ability to see the human in the other." Love, he said, "triumphs over systems," and is expressed in "petty acts of kindness."

I believe that if you can just stretch yourself a little and become slightly more empathetic, it is a huge accomplishment. The heart doesn't break, it stretches. When you have loss or grief, you get through it and can absorb more. There's a type of resilience that is learned.

The world is not a safe space. After I adopted my daughter, I took her to her little classroom. She had just recently come over from Russia. She barely spoke English. I remember holding her hand and gesturing telling her to go sit with the other kids in a circle. She went over and a boy got up and pushed her down on the floor. The teachers started to go over to pick her up and I made a gesture for them to stop. My daughter looked over at me and I gestured to her saying, "Get up, get up." I wanted to encourage her to stand up on her own. I wanted her to practice resilience.

Our struggle transcends these safe spaces, it transcends identity, and it must transcend the walls we use to close ourselves off. Our struggle is over an inarguable human right. Culture and politics must be secondary to this human right. We need Reproductive Freedom and Justice without borders.

Come Out, Come Out. Wherever You Are

For anyone wanting to become an activist, there are rallies and there are actions. There is a multiplicity of things that can be done. Many of these are listed and explained on the RiseUp website.[45]

---

45 https://riseup4abortionrights.org/

And there are many other organizations that one may feel more comfortable with that offer multiple ways of becoming involved. The real question that each of us must ask is: "what can I, realistically, do?"

After *Dobbs*, many people contacted us wanting to volunteer, wanting to do *something*. They would commit a few days and then call up and say, "I can't really do this." They don't have time. They can't march. But they are inspired. So, the goals have to be realistic and feasible. Exactly how much time do they have? Exactly what can you do?

Some humility is really needed here. In a sense, wanting to always do more than you can is a recipe for non-action, for passivity and despair. Always comparing ourselves to others, there is a tendency to believe that if you can't change the world by the power of your own personality immediately, you have failed. In reality, that is not possible. But you can change yourself and the people around you. In fact, each and every interaction is a workshop for change.

I am reminded of when I was very active in the animal rights movement, and I would be challenged by the Jacobians (purists) for wearing leather and not being a vegan, even though I was a vegetarian at the time. It's as if one can't do it all, you are failing some kind of purity test.

Participating in a march is wonderful. It can be inspiring and, in some cases, lead to long-term commitment. But in most cases, it does not. I always go back to Black Lives Matter. Often, I could see them marching outside my window and of course I followed all the action. The question I would ask myself and others was: why don't we have those kinds of numbers and that intensity for women's lives and freedom?

Is it that there is not enough of a visceral connection to the issue? Is it those "outposts in our heads," or perhaps that women are just not that important? Perhaps it is because the right to legal safe abortion has always been cast as a "women's issue." Perhaps it is because many women are risk averse and marching in the streets is inherently risky?

George Floyd was one man, but we all saw his horrendous murder and he came to personify police brutality. The Black Lives Matter movement was able to harness that galvanizing event and others like it to bring millions out to protest.

What about all the women and girls who have laid down their bodies in filthy places throughout the ages and died? Is it because women don't count? Years ago, at a large meeting I called for the New York Pro-Choice Coalition of providers, nonprofits, and supporting organizations, I urged them to focus on the death of so many women from illegal abortions—to perhaps catalyze compassion and rage. Yet, when we discussed using the iconic photograph of Gerri Santoro—in a motel room, hunched over so you only see her back, blood everywhere, dead from an illegal self-abortion—we were told, mainly by Planned Parenthood, not to use it because it was "too upsetting" and too negative. This is a major problem. Women die every day from illegal abortions. They have died all throughout history. There are stories—thousands of them—of the torture women have endured. But they do not resonate in the same way.

Perhaps it is that people don't care, or perhaps we have become totally desensitized: murder, another massacre, another school shooting, another hate crime. It's known as compassion fatigue.

And there is that feeling of impotence, of being unable to make a difference, of being a victim of forces beyond our control. But if we truly accept the fact that many of the circumstances in our lives are truly beyond our control and the only true thing we can control is our reaction to events, then we begin to learn the perspective required to continue to resist and act in the world.

I do things because I think they are the right things to do. I would like to see the results of my actions played out in the way I intended them, but I have no control over that part. If you live with that understanding, you become freer in your ability to act.

We must also hold elected officials' feet to the fire. They must know what is on the line for *them*. If they keep saying "vote for us" and we continue to vote for them and nothing changes, what message are we sending? No more feet up on desks.

Coming out of the abortion closet is a great contribution. Seventy percent of the country is pro-choice, according to the most recent polls, but the truth is that everybody is touched by this issue. If everyone who had an abortion, and all the men who were involved in these abortions, and every friend, relative, and acquaintance would say it, I project that almost all of us have been touched by abortion. The numbers would be extraordinary. We need to get out from under the shame and the stigma, which is the narrative of the opposition.

Women and girls are living in the urgency of now. Twenty-three million women in this country have absolutely no access to legal safe abortion. Will we allow that number to rise to 166 million and welcome this Brave New World of female breeders? Or will we answer the call of science, reason, compassion, human rights, and justice? I call on all people of conscience, especially young people, to resist this metastasis of misogynistic moral panic and act.

Start with the Parents

The role and participation of parents in education and the educational system has now become one of the poles that the culture wars are wrapped around. Florida is leading the competition to become the new Renaissance Florence. There, Governor Ron DeSantis has created his own bonfire of vanities. But rather than throwing objects like cosmetics, art, and books into a great roaring fire in the middle of Miami, he throws in any discussion of LGBTQ+ issues, trans issues, and critical race theory.

A modern-day Savonarola, DeSantis does not realize that burning is not the answer. As George Will pointed out in a 2023 column for the *Washington Post*, "Addressing a right to life gala last weekend, Florida Gov. Ron DeSantis emphatically reaffirmed—and more firmly impaled himself on—the bill he signed banning abortion after six weeks, a point at which many women do not know they are pregnant. He called it 'landmark' legislation that he was 'happy' to sign." Interesting that DeSantis used the word "landmark"—which is defined as a decision that establishes an important new legal principle. The six-week ban could be read as the "Establishment Clause" of DeSantis's new theocracy—defining when women are pregnant (electrical impulses that they call heartbeats) and placing them in the category of non-reasoning, reproducing bodies of the state.

We should start not with school systems, but with the parents. I believe that every parent wants to be the best they can be. They want to do everything they can for their children. And they would like their children to reflect what they consider to be their "best selves."

When it comes to abortion, much of the available material out there focuses on sex education and biology. This is because the argument itself has always been too focused on the act of abortion, and at this point, on the fetus—its rights and ability to feel—not abortion as an expression of the right to choose when and whether to parent.

In this country, we have certain rights, and the right to decide when we want to have children is one of them. I would encourage parents to talk to their children about the right to decide as much as the biology. An abortion is a physical act, but properly contextualized, it's about women's lives, freedom, and a fundamental civil and human right. And it is about women in context—the context of their families, their children, and their communities.

My daughter has grown up in this space. She started working at Choices when she was around thirteen years old. She is very familiar with the topic of abortion. She went through a period where she did not want to tell her friends what I did. And she went through a period of time when she said, "At Choices, you kill babies." I told her some people would say that, and she will read many things about me and my work that are very negative, which is complicated.

She came to me at one point and said, "I don't think I would ever have an abortion. If I got pregnant, I'd want to keep my baby." So, we had that conversation—about the many reasons why people get abortions and how important the choice is. I said, "If it is your choice, and if you want to have a child, I'll do everything to help and support you." However, I'm very clear on the essence of choice.

It's a difficult thing. A young child hears about abortion—that it is killing babies—and they don't want to kill anything. So, it is a complicated topic, and it requires a complicated conversation made simple. Abortion as the *process* of exercising the right to choose is what is lost so often lost in the fog of the abortion war. A person can be totally anti-abortion, but if they are not actively working to curtail the choice for all women, I consider that they are pro-choice. Once you start to expand your own moral and religious thinking to limit and control my choices, that is a different story. That context is important.

Another casualty of the "fog" of war is speaking truthfully about pregnancy and motherhood. Parents should be truthful about the dangers and costs of becoming pregnant and becoming a parent. Children should learn that giving birth is still a dangerous undertaking, particularly for poor Black and minority women. They should also be aware that the leading cause of death in pregnant women is homicide.[46]

Are we looking at yet another socially constructed binary? Is it just another iteration of the madonna/whore complex? Women who do not have abortions and give birth are the madonnas (although these conceptions are far from immaculate) and of course those who choose to abort—whores. The time has come to deconstruct this and move to a more fluid definition of choosing to parent. Indeed, the number of people deciding *not* to have children is rising.[47] Interestingly enough, they are looking at issues like climate change and economics in a far less romantic and traditional way.

---

46 Roni Caryn Rabin, "Maternity's Most Dangerous Time: After New Mothers Come Home," *New York Times*, May 28, 2023, https://www.nytimes.com/2023/05/28 /health/pregnancy-childbirth-deaths.html.

47 Anna Brown, "Growing Share of Childless Adults in U.S. Don't Expect to Ever Have Children," Pew Research Center, November 29, 2021, https://www.pewresearch .org/short-reads/2021/11/19/growing-share-of-childless-adults-in-u-s-dont-expect-to -ever-have-children/.

How do you normalize the conversation? In a sense, everyone is talking about abortion, but in bumper stickers, hyperbolic terms—in slogans. We have not regularized the *real* conversation yet. It is crucial that we do. We must tell our abortion stories and listen to others'. I encourage people to carefully broach the subject, to find out where a person's thoughts are. What they think about it. Do they know anyone who had an abortion? It requires a bit of psychological courage, but it is a good way to come out of the abortion closet and to bring others out.

Start with the understanding that we must always accept the other and their way of being in the world. You have to accept that somebody will say, "I would never do this. You are killing an innocent being." You have to have able to say, "I understand, and I would never force you to make that decision." The question is *who* gets to make that choice? Someone will. Nothing will stop abortion. The only difference is that when abortion is illegal, women will suffer and die.

If you haven't had the conversation, it's not an easy one. It likely will surprise the parties involved because so many people will share that they knew that their mothers or grandmothers or a woman in their life had an abortion, or almost had an abortion. Many will talk about Aunt So and So, who was always discussed in whispers because she had had more than one, and perhaps died of one.

When I started to go around the country and debate and give speeches, invariably, one or two or three women would come up to me and say, "I never told anybody this, but I had an abortion." People will talk to me about that, which is encouraging. Of course, I'd like it screamed in the streets. A girl can *dream*, but I really want to wake everyone up!

There are embers in all these women. Maybe there was a passionate affair, or they had to make a decision about abortion and the repressed anger was smoldering. Life interferes and not everyone can go out and march. Maybe they are intimidated to speak out publicly. That is the bonfire I want to build from all those embers. I want to tell women to own their decision, to give voice to that fury.

Now, parents need to have yet another difficult conversation with their daughters. Similar to the conversation Black mothers and fathers have with their sons about how to act when they are walking down the street and they see police coming in their direction, mothers and fathers will have to talk with their daughters about access to abortion and how geography will determine access. It will impact their lives. They will have to know that *where* they live will affect *how* they live. According to Jessica Valenti in her *Abortion Everyday* blog on Substack, 72 percent of college students say abortion law could impact their decision to remain in school.

We are seeing those decisions already being taken into account when it comes to choosing a college or university. According to a BestColleges survey conducted in July 2022, "abortion access has become an increasingly influential consideration in students' college decisions."

"Of those planning to enroll in an undergraduate program sometime in the next twelve months, 39 percent said that the court's decision to overturn *Roe v. Wade* will affect their decision to attend college in a particular state. Similarly, 43 percent of current undergrads said that the overturning of *Roe v. Wade* has led them to question whether they want to remain in the state where they are attending college or transfer elsewhere."[48]

This is such a dynamic reality. Every day is another lawsuit, another attempt to restrict abortion somewhere. Ideally, this should be a civics lesson, but we don't teach civics anymore. What does it mean to live in this democratic republic? All the founders imagined their extraordinary project with the participation of an educated and engaged citizenry.

---

48 Morgan Smith, "Gen Z is re-thinking college and career plans in post-Roe America: 'I want to leave the country'," CNBC, December 19, 2022, https://www.cnbc.com/2022/12/19/gen-z-on-new-college-and-career-plans-in-post-roe-america.html.

The Role of Men

In the early days, many women asked, "Don't you realize legal abortion will let men off the hook completely?" Before *Roe*, if a man got a woman pregnant, they would have a shotgun wedding and do "the honorable thing." But how many of those marriages ended in divorce or abandonment? And do we even have a definition of honor that the majority can agree on?

We're in a different world now, and there has been a lot of thoughtful writing on what is happening with men and where they stand in relation to women and to themselves. The increase in depression, aggression, "deaths of despair," and young men who define themselves as "incels" (short for "involuntarily celibate") are indices that tell an alarming story. The new male "gurus" like Canadian psychologist Jordan Peterson and right-wing activist Matt Walsh offer different definitions incorporating the values of protection, growth, and mastery.

Feminist politics must truly begin at home, in relation to the other—and many times, it must be in bed. Since *Dobbs,* there has been a 29 percent increase in vasectomy requests nationwide.[49] Many of these men are partnered and have wisely chosen a permanent sterilization procedure to ensure protection. Vasectomies are outpatient permanent sterilization procedures that block sperm from being released in semen. They are also less invasive than tubal ligation and have a far lower failure rate than many other types of contraception, including condoms and the pill.

When we speak about the role of men, it is often within the context of the abortion decision itself—as partners, as half of the creators of the pregnancy. I did many debates in the eighties and nineties with men who were demanding to have not only a legally established role in the abortion decision, but a veto over it. The man may not have legal veto power in a decision, but

---

49 Carolyn Crist, "Vasectomy Requests Increase After Roe Ruling," WebMD, June 30, 2022, https://www.webmd.com/men/news/20220630/vasectomy-requests-increase -after-roe

their influence on that decision is heavily dependent on not only their relationship with the woman, but how they view the role of "father."

Guido Reichstader, the RiseUp activist who chained himself to the gates in front of the Supreme Court and went on a hunger strike when he was arrested, spoke eloquently of the perils facing young women in this moment and his definition of a father's role.

> The Supreme Court is engaged in an unconstitutional attack on the rights of women in this country. . . . I've got a twelve-year-old daughter—I'm willing to go to bat for her rights, I'm willing to do whatever it takes. Young people—you deserve the right to make decisions about your own bodies. That right is inalienable; they can't take that right away; all they can do is punish you for exercising it. Young people, y'all have the power and the courage. The old people have had it beaten out of them over the years.

Now, men must be brought into the public political conversation. They certainly have not been silent on the issue, passing one law after another while not even having the slightest idea of female physiology, let alone psychology. One wonders how many of these men's wives, girlfriends, and mistresses were patients at abortion clinics. I know I have seen quite a few at mine.

I used to laugh when it became common for people to say, "We are pregnant." The question back then was: what percentage of men are not paying alimony or need child support?

Now, with *Dobbs*, the question is: would Republicans pursue the death penalty for men who impregnate abortion-seeking women?

Men may now have a conversation with the women they are having sex with about the possibilities of criminal action if she decides to have an abortion. In a moving article for *Time* called "My Wife's Abortion Taught Me About Civil Rights," Ariel Chesler—a judge, writer, and the son of feminist author and psychologist Phyllis Chesler—wrote of growing up surrounded by activism:

I learned the importance of respecting the agency of women and their right to make moral choices. But, as I marched and spoke about these issues, it was always from an intellectual and emotional distance. Sure, my mother had spoken to me about having abortions, and I understood that the issue of abortion could touch the women in my life—my friends, my wife, my daughters—but it was always theoretical.

When he and his wife learned eighteen weeks into their third pregnancy that it had become nonviable, he wrote that "[t]he theoretical quickly became real and personal. When my wife's doctors recommended terminating the pregnancy, although we were deeply saddened at the loss of the new life we had expected to add to our family, we knew that the most moral choice was abortion. We were comforted by the fact that my wife had choices. More important, she had choices which were accessible, safe and affordable, unlike a growing number of women in our country."[50]

This kind of understanding is crucial. Men have a role to play, and it's important to recognize that role.

At Choices, men who accompanied their partners to abortion appointments would receive pamphlets that included a synopsis of the procedure, information on aftercare (not having vaginal intercourse for two weeks after a follow-up appointment), and which stressed the need for understanding, love, and support. If they wanted, they could speak to a counselor.

Once, a patient came with her fiancé, and before the appointment, the fiancé called and said he wanted to propose as soon as she got out of the recovery room. He said, "I love her and I'm there for her. Can you help me?" So, we did. We got flowers and we coordinated the whole thing. We played her favorite song and as she walked down from the second floor to the first, there he was, flowers in his hand. He went down on one knee and proposed right there. They came back later to have their child with us.

However, men must understand that the decision is ultimately

---

50 Ariel Chesler, "My Wife's Abortion Taught Me About Civil Rights," *Time*, March 2, 2016, https://time.com/4243627/my-wifes-abortion/.

a woman's decision. She has veto power. Still, it is important to involve somebody in a conversation about the results of an intimate act, about the creation or potential creation of a child in this universe.

Love and Death

As a reaction to liberal feminism, the eighties also saw the development of difference feminism, which emphasized the similarities between women and men in order to argue for equal treatment for women. At the same time, the AIDS epidemic was raging, causing oceans of anxiety, despair, and death. The issue was argued politically, medically, and philosophically. Susan Sontag used it as a focus of social critique. Illness as a metaphor. It had shades of the medieval black plague. It was controversial, dangerous, and it was profound.

The profundity touched me one morning when I was dressing and listening to the radio. It was an interview with a Shanti counselor on the AIDS ward. She was saying something extraordinary, something that made me pause in my daily ritual. Working with AIDS patients made her realize that if she would choose her own death, she would want to know she was dying. For one year, she would want to experience the clarity, the restructuring of priorities, the immediate placement of things important and not so important that she witnessed through working with some of her patients.

Then, of course, there was the sexuality issue; the fact that a large majority of the AIDS patients were male homosexuals—an easy target for the right-wing ideologues. The AIDS epidemic was Jerry Falwell's proof that God was punishing our society for its decadence. Not only was abortion a blight that befell the sinners, but now the Deity had something even worse in the offing: the "Gay Plague."

AIDS was the gay man's unwanted pregnancy. The epidemic showed the world for the first time that a man's sexual life could cost him his future and his life.

And then there was Calvin, my hairdresser. The strangeness had gone on for about a year. I would be called and told that he could not make appointments or would have to be late. He started to look thinner and thinner. I would question him, but he just said he wasn't feeling well, some stomach problems or something. Then one day, as I was sitting in his chair, while he went through his programmatic cosmetic rituals, I looked up into the mirror and caught his eye and again asked him what was wrong. He didn't answer verbally, but he answered. I knew at that moment that he had AIDS, and I also knew that he was dying.

At the time, AIDS was exploding, and San Francisco General Hospital was where many of the early patients were being treated. I knew I had to go there.

When I arrived at the San Francisco airport, I immediately took a cab to San Francisco General. When I got to Ward 86, they were expecting me. Yes, they would let Dr. Kaplan know that I was there. Two men were seated at phone desks, perhaps using a generic script. Phrases like "no, you can't catch it by being in the same room; yes, we do have community support systems"—intense, involved, caring. I sat down in front of them. In a strange way I felt comfortable, safe. I felt that I could trust these people.

Dr. Kaplan came out to greet me. I was referred to him through a contact in New York. He would be my guide, my connection to the world on ward 86.

We started in his office, a small, partitioned cubicle. He told me about his work, how being an oncologist got him used to his patients dying—sort of. How the research didn't have the answers—yet. How much the medical staff depended on the support systems generated by the gay community and the city of San Francisco. How on some days it was horrible—when they had about sixty patients in the last stages of the disease coming in weekly for treatment. How he had to deal with the depression, the rage, the incredible unbelievable reality of thirty-year-old men dying.

I asked him about medication—anti-depressants. They didn't use them. After all, the reality was that they did have a fatal illness

(50 percent of patients diagnosed with AIDS were terminal)—what could drugs do for that? I asked about his own depression. He said it was difficult.

For Dr. Gary Kaplan, dealing with the dying AIDS patients helped him cope with his own anxiety about getting AIDS. He felt that if in fact he was ever diagnosed with AIDS, it would be easier for him to deal with it because he was involved in helping others do the same. Maybe.

Then there was his bike and the hills of San Francisco. That was his therapy. The rides alone in the hills when there was one phone call too many, one Bobbi too many.

Gary asked me whether I wanted to go into the inpatient area, the place where the final stages of this deadly drama played out. I wanted to see it, to be there, so we walked through the green hospital corridors together until we reached the area. There were only twelve beds. Outside of each room a bright pink poster entitled INFECTIOUS PRECAUTIONS listed directions for staff dealing with the patients—a check-off system:

- MASK
- GOWN
- GLOVES
- PUNCTURE
- PROOF
- NEEDLE BOX IN ROOM
- NO PREGNANT WOMEN

And then there was the room with the handwritten sign outside that read: NO FLOWERS.

No flowers. It was then I felt I wanted to cry.

The literature rack told volumes. Brochures such as "Coping with AIDS!" "Getting Your Affairs in Order," "A Bridge of Love and Affirmation," "When a Friend Has AIDS," "Affection Not Rejection"—these spoke to the love and support of the staff for these patients.

All the workers on this ward were volunteers, and most of

them were gay. I asked whether their sexual orientation was the primary reason for their wanting to work on this ward.

"Not the only reason, but it's important."

The issue of this disease—AIDS—had galvanized the gay community and had created networks of ancillary support systems that reached out to the established medical community, surrounded it and supported and changed the conventional avenues of medical treatment.

A visual flash—the end of a bed—a thin, almost skeletal leg sticking out of the white bed sheets—spasmodically twitching— the door partly open—someone sitting at the bedside.

And then I felt the rage—one lives one's life making choices that challenge the established order, struggling to self-actualize, to break free of barriers that don't fit.

Loving and touching and experiencing—planning futures— paying bills—living in and out of the societal norms—and one morning just like any other morning, coffee, a cigarette—the daily rituals that give comfortable habitual structure—minor anchors.

Then, suddenly, your throat hurts—or you realize that you've been tired too long—or there's the feeling that the gland in your neck is swollen. One morning/afternoon—or anytime—your world radically changes. And there is no reason. And yet there is.

Gary told me that his experience of working with dying patients showed him that "angry people die angry and actualized people grow more."

As if AIDS were an enormous challenge—facing death, learning to cope—reaching that acceptance level was something that not all attained.

Gary's rage would come at a strange time. It would come when one of his patients finally came to the point of acceptance—and would tell him "I'm ready—I'm not fighting anymore." Then Gary would take to his bike—take to the hills—as if their acceptance were his failure.

When we came back to the outpatient ward, Gary was called to the phone. More instructions—more bad news to give.

A patient passed by, supported by a staff member—thin,

walking haltingly—and I knew that I was there for a moment in time that would be repeated again and again.

I didn't disturb Gary—the connecting line was too important. I touched his shoulder as I left, feeling the specialness of these people.

Calvin died the week after I left San Francisco.

Was he accepting? Or was it more of a gentle struggle?

Did Calvin remember my caring?

The only thing I can think of now is that I hope wherever he was, they let him have flowers.

CHAPTER 10
LOVE

Creating Windows

"Patient #4 in recovery was moved by your work and wants to see you."

When my assistant's email came through, I was in the middle of a meeting in my office. Excusing myself, I put on the white coat I always keep hanging on the back of my chair and went up to the recovery room.

In the fourth bed, I met the wide dark eyes of the woman who wanted to see me and introduced myself. She reached out her arms, and as I drew her close to me her words spilled out.

"You saved my life. I was eighteen weeks—the baby was dead—they should have told me weeks ago. The doc—she didn't want to help. I found you on the internet—read all about you. Why didn't they tell me earlier? You saved me—thank you, thank you."

As we embraced, I thanked her for reminding me why I have spent the last fifty years of my life doing this work. When I left her bedside, I grabbed her chart to get the whole story from the counselor's notes:

Caucasian patient was 18 weeks pregnant with a planned pregnancy. While receiving pre-natal care she was informed, two weeks ago, about fetal abnormalities indicating severe developmental issues. Patient told to return in two weeks and seek an abortion independently. No assistance was offered. Patient was severely upset because the same abnormality had been confirmed with a prior pregnancy of 9 weeks gestation leading to a much easier termination process. Patient became familiar with Merle Hoffman and her activism on the Internet and became teary eyed during session when describing what Ms. Hoffman's work meant to her, and later inquired about the possibility of meeting Ms. Hoffman personally.

The great Persian poet Rumi wrote: "When the house of the world is dark, love will find a way to create windows."

Darkness is a perfect metaphor for ignorance, which takes you away from the light; away from enlightenment; away from love, open-mindedness, reality, and experience. All of us must choose to be present. That is our responsibility—to be awake to the realities of life.

We live in a moment of great danger and challenge. How we respond to this personally and nationally is utterly critical to the lives of women and girls around the globe. This country has been an example in the worldwide struggle for women's equality and humanity. With the overturning of *Roe*, we have lost that credibility—but we must individually and communally take up the mantle of responsibility to regain it.

Yes, in our struggle for freedom, the movement must be like the phoenix. However many times we are reduced to ashes, we must Rise Up from the embers of our dreams and the remains of what we once were to begin again—more powerful, and wiser than before.

What is it that will enable us to put our lives on the line as the women in Latin America have done in a decades-long struggle to win decriminalization of abortion in the most Catholic and conversative of countries or as the brave women in Iran, who as I write are being killed in the streets as they struggle for freedom from the religious and autocratic misogynist oppression?

Che Guevara said, "At the risk of seeming ridiculous, let me say that the true revolutionary is guided by a great feeling of love. It is impossible to think of a genuine revolutionary lacking this quality." So, what is the love that drives these women to put their lives on the line for a mission, a cause, a deep primal belief in something that transcends the self, and for moments in time truly can go beyond ego?

I firmly believe that anyone who stands for truth and justice is a radical and revolutionary, and operates on feelings of love. As I have said, and have been attacked for, many times: Choosing to have an abortion is often an act of love and always an act of survival.

There is a choice in love, in how we love and how we define love.

The Sami people in Northern Russia and Finland have 180 words for snow, so deep is their understanding of it. The Greeks had a number of words for "love" in all of its meanings—familiar love, sacrificial love, etc. These reflect a far more sensitized experience and understanding of love: "eros" for physical love or sexual desire; "philia" for friendship; "agape" for unconditional, selfless, sacrificial love; "storge" for familial love; "mania" for obsessive love.

How many words do we have for love? We love everything, but what does it mean to love a person in the same way that we "love" baseball, for example? What are we surrounded by? Division, hate, envy, resentment.

This is why active loving is so important. How do you help a person who is coming to you in crisis, with an unwanted pregnancy? They have something happening that has the power to radically alter their future. You have to contextualize it for them to make them feel comfortable, supported, and give them compassion. This is love. Elie Wiesel once told me:

> There is no real definition of love, for once you define it disappears. The act of trying to define it diminishes it. It is a mystery, but it is a kind of identification with another person where that other person is as important as yourself and that person's life as important as yours. It means that I would exchange my life for hers. Does it mean sacrifice? Not at all. It means offering. Love is that. Every gesture becomes an offering.

Perhaps Wiesel is using the word "offering" in the biblical sense—an act of gratitude to God. I would use this in a secular sense to urge us to focus on gratitude for the gift of being able to be active, and capable of offering your time, passion, energy, anger, and focus on an issue that is so fundamental to more than half of this world's population, which is why it is a privilege to be part of this great social movement and struggle.

And Yet...

In the days since *Dobbs*, I have thought often of the dialogue I had with Elie Wiesel. I asked him: "If God's divinity is expressed through humanity and ultimately through love, and, as you have said many times, 'Everything died in Auschwitz,' how can we expect love to save us?" His response was:

> My favorite words are "and yet."
> Everything died in Auschwitz . . . and yet.
> Yes, there are reasons for me to despair . . . and yet.
> Yes, there are reasons for me not to believe in God and yet . . .
> And yet . . .

To act on love requires the courage to say "and yet"—to take that "leap of faith," as Kierkegaard says. Love is a positive emotion, a desire to move out of yourself, to be compassionate, to show radical empathy. Love must be what drives us—toward action, toward truth, toward resistance.

I often think of a patient we had at Choices not long ago. She was twenty weeks pregnant and was told by her doctor that the fetus had a terrible condition, and that survival outside of the womb would be almost impossible.

After a long, difficult discussion, she decided to terminate the pregnancy. But she had a request: She wanted an impression of the fetus's feet. Our staff at Choices had seen many rituals associated with abortion over the years, but this was the first time a patient requested a footprint.

We arranged for the impression to be made. We respected it and understood. It was an act of compassion—an act of love.

EPILOGUE
THE ABYSS GAZES BACK

When the Supreme Court effectively overturned *Roe v. Wade* with the *Dobbs* decision in June 2022, I thought I knew what a catastrophe for women, girls, and women's health care it would be. But as we enter the second year of living with *Dobbs* and its progeny, the consequences appear far worse and more expansive than I could have predicted.

As I was writing this book, wrestling with broad historical, legal, and philosophical themes, I was bombarded daily—in my clinic, in the news, by word-of-mouth—with an unrelenting avalanche of examples of the cruel and draconian realities of life under *Dobbs*. It reminded me of the summer I spent so many years ago immersing myself in the literature of the Holocaust. I would think I had read everything about the camps and the cruelty, and that it could not possibly get worse. But I was always wrong. With each new book, new research paper, or primary source, it would just get worse. It was in the nuances, the stories of the survivors, that the evil would be personalized. Eventually, it occurred to me that there was no bottom to this abyss and that what Nietzsche said was true: "If you gaze long enough into an abyss, the abyss will gaze back into you."

For over a year now, I have looked deeply and painfully into the abyss of the *Dobbs* decision. Staring back at me are the faces of the women and girls who will be forced to endure unnecessary cruelty and tragedy under this barbaric patchwork of laws. Women like the unidentified Wisconsin patient who was left to bleed at home when, out of fear that they might violate the state's abortion ban, the hospital staff would not remove the fetal tissue from an incomplete miscarriage; Elizabeth Weller, who, after her water broke too early for the fetus to survive, was not offered an abortion, but was instead sent home from a Texas hospital until she showed signs of infection; Samantha Casiano, who was forced to carry a fetus with a fatal anomaly to term because she was unable to pay the cost of leaving the state; Delmy Chavez, who worried she would be accused of murder after an emergency surgery to address internal bleeding caused by an ectopic pregnancy; or Amanda Zurawski, who developed sepsis and nearly died due to doctors delaying an abortion. The list goes on. These are the stories we hear about, stories of women nearly dying, women being denied care, women having to travel across state lines, physicians afraid of criminal prosecution—a terrifying, ever-evolving landscape of cruelty. These are the stories of the abortion war survivors.

There are no doubt hundreds of women with stories like these, many of whom do not have the means to file lawsuits, reach out to reporters, or have their voices heard. They will suffer their tragedies in silence. These are the causalities, the necessary "sacrifices" made on the way towards the utopian "pro-life" vision in which abortion will be unthinkable and unimaginable.

Let's think about and imagine this:

As I write these final words, the South Carolina Supreme Court upheld a strict six-week abortion ban, writing that they were leaving "for another day" a decision on when the fetal heartbeat limit began during pregnancy. And again, we must ask: Is there not a heart beating in every woman?

"Doctors practicing under the strict law cannot similarly punt on that question," noted James Pollard of the *Associated Press*. "Physicians say the statute's unclear guidance is already chilling medical practice at the few abortion clinics that operate in the conservative state. With potential criminal charges hanging in the balance, most abortions are being halted as doctors wrestle with the murky legal definitions."

And this:

A male MAGA judge was recently quoted as saying that the abortion pill "robs doctors of the joy of seeing fetal photos," projecting a hypothetical emotional reaction onto unknown doctors. This is no longer merely a case of the enemy having "outpost in our heads," it is a complete invasion. Stories such as those above can only be described as torture.

We are now in the midst of a human rights crisis. As *Dobbs* denies individual women the ability to use their reason (which I have described in this book as that which makes us human), it is nothing less than our basic human rights that are being violated. In terms of religious freedom—*Dobbs* is based on a fundamentalist Catholic belief that life begins at conception—the Supreme Court has minimized or totally rejected the beliefs of other faiths. Digital incursions into medical records and personal social media platforms, common in the *Dobbs* era, are flagrant violations of our rights to privacy and egregious assaults on the patient-doctor relationship.

Indeed, this country is in violation of multiple signed international treaties that forbid a great deal of what has been happening to women as the result of *Dobbs*. But let us not forget that this country has a long history of segregating entire populations for second-class treatment. When Nazi Germany passed the Nuremberg Laws in 1935, they looked to us. "America in the early Twentieth Century," wrote James Q. Whitman, author of *Hitler's American Model*, "was the leading racist jurisdiction in the world."

As we move deeper into the *Dobbs* era and we find ourselves keeping score, state by state, on abortion, let us remember that any state victories we celebrate are Pyrrhic victories. How long will we allow ourselves to be distracted by state-level election activity and coverage? How long will we be reporting on casualty after casualty of this war? How long will we fill the internet with words before we realize it is the streets we must fill—with rage? How long until every single one of us takes responsibility for where we are and where we are going?

Upon sending this book to press, I received word that Mexico has decriminalized abortion nationwide. This effort is part of a broader coalition of Latin American countries working to bolster women's rights, including Colombia, Argentina, Uruguay, and Guyana. All of these changes are due to the longtime struggle and opposition orchestrated by participants in the Green Wave over the last ten years. Some of them worked with RiseUp and were integral to our situational success.

We must look and learn from people like these, who have so courageously and consistently become a human wave of demand and resistance until they made change happen. *How long will it take for this to happen here?* Let us now look into our mirrors and our hearts and finally realize that it is only us—each and every one of us—who have the answer to that question.

ACKNOWLEDGMENTS

As this book was written in the midst of the *Dobbs* fallout, my first and deepest thanks and gratitude go to my staff at Choices, who, after dealing with the residue of the Pandemic, had to facilitate the influx of patients coming from "slave states" that had either banned or restricted abortion services. No matter the daily (and often hourly challenges), they have continued to actualize the vision and mission of Choices.

To Dr. Jay Bassell, Dr. Evans Crevecouer, Dr. Gerald Zupnick, and Dr. George McMillan, who have all been with me an average of twenty years, your commitment and service to all of Choices' patients are an example of what it truly means to embody the highest ideals of a physician, and I applaud you for having the courage and fortitude to continue to do so in a war zone. A shout out to Dr. Joseph Ottolenghi, who has just joined our staff and is such an important part of our future.

A very special thanks to my wartime Business Development consigliere, Carmine Asparro, for having my back for over forty years.

My appreciation and praise for three amazingly loyal and talented individuals who have exhausted themselves in filling multiple roles and functions, to "be there for me and Choices" in these exceedingly challenging times: Kelly Mallinson, my CAO who has been with me for eighteen years, balancing a toddler at home with a four-hour commute; Lorna Aguilos, a seventeen-year veteran, who is balancing grandchildren with a four-hour commute, and Sotiria Peppas, seven years and counting, my assistant who has courageously rose to the occasion of facilitating the multiplicity of edits for this book and worked at the speed of a demon.

I want to express my deep appreciation and gratitude for the team of professionals who have been my guides, allies, and great interlocutors along the way:

To Richard Rubenstein, a public relations guru and an old friend who came back into my life after working with me on many of my radical actions in the 1980s, for suggesting that I do this book and for bringing me to Skyhorse.

To Tony Lyons, publisher of Skyhorse, whose heterodox thinking and brave entrepreneurship welcomed me into his publishing family with open arms.

To Mark Gompertz, who understood my reality and worked closely with me to develop an individualized, creative structure to accommodate my writing from a war zone.

To my editors Jon Arlan and Jesse McHugh, with whom I have spent these last eight months in a continuous, challenging, political, philosophical conversation, where they learned about the intricacies and history of feminism and abortion, and I learned how to communicate my thoughts on the page in a less free-associative and esoteric way. Our editing discussions were always respectful, challenging, and sometimes a lot of fun—I will truly miss them.

To Rachel Marble, for her efforts on Skyhorse's end to help publicize and market the book.

To Karen Gantz, my attorney who handled the process of negotiations with Skyhorse with grace.

To all those who worked and struggled in joy and resistance in the year of RiseUp: Lori Sokol, long-time feminist, friend, sister-in-arms, and editor of *Women's E-News* who worked with me with passion and commitment; Sunsara Taylor, committed activist, organizer, speaker; Chantelle Hershberger, the photo curator for this book, website guru, organizer; Samantha Goldman, fundraiser, organizer; Patricia Wallin, storyteller and international organizer; and all the wonderful long-time and virgin activists who worked with me in the streets.

To Marylou Greenberg, who has participated with me in so many battles over thirty years, as well as being an editor and contributor of *On the Issues* and developing the Escort Program at Choices.

To Joan Roth, an indefatigable photographer who was at every one of RiseUp's rallies and marches and captured the energy and drama of it all.

To Carolyn Handel, who was so instrumental in helping me to take *On the Issues* from Choices in-house Newsletter to a glossy quarterly international magazine which at its height had sixteen thousand subscribers.

And for those who share not only my political life but my personal as well:

To Phyllis Chesler, my decades-long comrade-in-arms, confidant, sister warrior, and political soulmate, whose feminist activism, leadership, and literary output is legendary, and whose mentorship throughout this publishing process was invaluable.

To my dear friend Linda Stein, an exceptional artist whose many works on gender fluidity and anti-bullying adorn the walls of Choices, and who told me I was crazy for even thinking of doing this book, but always believed I could, and continually supported me through this process.

And finally, to my daughter, Sasharina (my unicorn), my deep love and gratitude for having to put up with Choices taking up so much of my life and has stretched herself even further to accommodate this book.